I Stand Amazed!
...At the Wonder of It All

by
Linda Schott

20th Century Christian
2809 Granny White Pike • Nashville, TN 37204

ISBN 0-89098-133-7

Giver of life, creator of all that is lovely,
    Teach me to sing the words to your song;
I want to feel the music of living
    And not fear the sad songs
But from them make new songs
    Composed of both laughter and tears.

Teach me to dance to the sounds of your world
    and your people,
I want to move in rhythm with your plan.
    Help me to try to follow your leading
To risk even falling
    To rise and keep trying
Because you are leading
    the joyous celebration
        dance of life.

Author unknown

Dedicated in memory of my father, Keith B. Kannard, from whom I inherited an indomitable spirit of optimism, joy and celebration. His death, when I was only four, left me forever changed, but his legacy lives on eternally in my heart...

And to my mother, Elizabeth Kannard, who gave me the most precious gift of childhood—the freedom to be a child—to dream, and to pursue those dreams...and to be ever amazed at the miracle of life.

With special thanks to my husband, Ken, for helping with research, for bearing with me through writer's block and computer blitz, and for endless patience, perseverance, and love.

Contents

I Stand Amazed!

Chapter 1:   . . .At the Wonder of It All 9

Chapter 2:   . . .At God the Father..................................19

Chapter 3:   . . .At the Glory of the Creation 29

Chapter 4:   . . .At the Promises of God..........................37

Chapter 5:   . . .At the Incarnation of Christ....................49

Chapter 6:   . . .At Jesus, the Messiah............................59

Chapter 7:   . . .At the Grace of God 71

Chapter 8:   . . .At the Word and Its Work 81

Chapter 9:   . . .At the Spirit, God's Special Gift 93

Chapter 10: . . .At Love, the Greatest Gift 103

Chapter 11: . . .At the Glory of God's Church 113

Chapter 12: . . .At the Hope of Heaven 121

Chapter 13: . . .At the Beauty of Praise and Worship ...133

Endnotes 143

Chapter 1

I Stand Amazed...
at the Wonder of It All

There are times in life when the mystery and splendor of God fill me with an irresistible knowledge and reassurance that God is sweeping into the deepest secret place of my being. His powerful presence fills me with amazement and replaces the dragging and often discordant melody of my life with a new song. It might be as I contemplate the wonders of nature, or feel the sweet softness of a newborn baby. It might be as I experience the magnificent poetry of the Psalms, or lift up a loved one in prayer.

At other times God seems farther away than the dimmest star on a summer evening. Apathy threatens to choke out my usual enthusiastic vigor, and my emotions and senses are dulled to even the most spectacular miracles of life. Bible reading becomes dull and monotonous, sermons uninteresting, and worship something to be tolerated.

In such valleys as these I hunger for spiritual renewal. I long to rekindle the dying embers of my faith and once again look with amazement at the power and grandeur of God as He plays out His master plan for mankind.

What happens between stage one—enthusiasm and enlightenment—and stage two—spiritual apathy? What forces pull us from the center and soul of our being and steal away the very breath of the spirit?

Most importantly, how do we return to the beginning of it all—the day we began our walk with Jesus Christ? How do we reclaim the vibrant and joyous wonder of an abundant life in Christ?

Misplaced Wonder

We've become a people programmed to take life for granted, and we find it easy to toss aside the miracle of the Gospel and bury it under the tenets of life in the fast-paced, technological, advanced 90's.

Life in this century IS spectacular. Things are changing at a faster pace than ever before in history. With each new dawn an exciting drug has been invented; a new technological breakthrough or scientific discovery makes the headlines.

Colonies in space, video telephones, and laser discs will be a thing of the past for our grandchildren. They will have access to such things as:

> Electronic malls
> ten-digit telephone numbers
> lap-top copiers
> microwave clothes dryers
> a "smart" house that controls all indoor functions with one tiny button
> self-weeding lawns![1]

Newly discovered knowledge is everywhere, and we stand in awe at the brilliance of man and his myriad accomplishments. But that doesn't change the basic premise of Christianity. We must get a grasp on the wondrous things of God before we drown in a sea of change. We need to once again sense the wonder of it all.

Sing It Over Again To Me

Does the story of Jesus still stir your heart? Does the Cross fill you with humble gratitude? Do you marvel at the certain knowledge that God is working in your life? Or, like so many others, have you ceased to be amazed?

One of the greatest tragedies of the world is that so many have not heard the story of Jesus. Equally distressing is the knowledge that an equal number of us consider Him to be merely commonplace. If you are the age of thirty, you've probably heard and digested at least 4,060 sermons and Bible studies over a twenty-year span. You've taken the Lord's Supper over 1,000 times. You've sung at least 15,600 songs! Add to that your personal devotions, family studies, vacation Bible schools, meetings, special Ladies' classes, etc., and the total equals a phenomenal number of times you've been exposed to the story of the Gospel!

We think because we've studied it a lifetime that we know and really understand the full significance of His life within us and among us—when in reality we have only touched the tip of the iceberg.

Robert M. Brown begins a chapter of his book *The Bible Speaks to You*, with a scroll on which are written the following words:

> BE IT HEREBY ENACTED:
> That every three years all people
> Shall forget whatever they have learned
> About Jesus,
> And begin the study all over again.

What Mr. Brown is really saying is that familiarity blunts the senses. The wonder has been lost because we've begun the study repeatedly, reading the printed word but not really seeing the true wonder; hearing the message but not comprehending; never searching yet deeper for new meanings to light the way. We've traveled the route of exploration in a type of semi-coma!

Read the words in 2 Peter 1:12-15:

> So I will always remind you of these things, even though you know them and are firmly established in the truth you now have. I think it is right to refresh your memory as long as I live in the tent of this body, because I know that I will soon put it aside, as our Lord Jesus Christ has made clear to me. And I will make every effort to see that after my departure you will always be able to remember these things.

Yes, you are already "firmly established in the truth you now have." However, my prayer is that this study will inspire within you a hungering desire to taste anew the sweetness and freshness of a walk with Christ, and that you'll be able to "sing a new song" to the Lord, for "He has done marvelous things" (Psa. 98:1).

In spite of the fact that the territory is familiar, I want you to experience renewal—to stand on the mountain and gaze with wonder upon fresh vistas of our Father's great plan. I want you to once again find inspiration in the simple songs of life. This time around, attempt to see the miracle of life in a new light—as though you were experiencing it for the first time.

A New Song

It almost sounds simplistic and Pollyannish. "Life isn't like that!" you say. "My burdens are great, the demands on my time are unlimited, and I really don't think things will ever change. I'm stuck in a rut and can't dig myself out!"

Before you label me as a "dreamer" who knows nothing of reality, let me hasten to say that the journey of my life has not been without pain. I have passed through many seasons with deafened ears and blinded sight. Never seeing the miracle of life which surrounded me, I was closed to the wonder of it all.

My purpose in writing this book is not to diminish the awfulness of tragedy, pain and affliction, but rather to help you understand (and to remind myself!) that we can rise above it and see beyond it to the wild and tenacious vividness of life. We can once again see the beauty and dignity of the human season and each life happening.

Choose Joy

Nehemiah wrote in 8:10, "The joy of the Lord is my strength." As I have attempted to unravel the truth of this scripture, it has revealed to me once again a touch of wonder at a life that is sacred. Joy is a gift and a privilege that I cannot comprehend. In spite of Satan's conspiracy to dash me against the solid rocks of a mammoth cliff and sling me in broken pieces to the depths of the roaring seas below, I have found joy and wonder, and it has given me strength.

At any difficult moment in life, we have at least two options. We can fold like the pleats of an accordion and silence the song, or we can embrace with all our being an attitude of gratitude for the endless free gifts that life offers and commit to a life of joy. I can turn my mourning into dancing, and my sackcloth into joy (Psa. 30:11). Put more simply, I can be a victim or a fighter.

I have made a deliberate choice to continue to gaze with wonder on the abundant blessings in Christ in spite of the pain. The joy I have chosen has not depended on circumstances, but instead it has existed in spite of difficulties that were undeniably real and painful.

> Though the fig tree does not bud
> and there are no grapes on the vines,
> though the olive crop fails
> and the fields produce no food,
> though there are no sheep in the pen
> and no cattle in the stalls,
> yet will I rejoice in the Lord,
> I will be joyful in God my Savior.
> The Sovereign Lord is my strength;
> he makes my feet like the feet of a deer,
> he enables me to go on the heights.
> Habakkuk 3:17-19

I have reason to rejoice and to catch the wonder of it all, in spite of overwhelming odds, because God is with me. When I'm suffering, either physically or emotionally, I try to remember to focus more on what I CAN do than what I CANNOT, more on the privilege of being alive than on circumstances which threaten to steal the very life of my spirit.

> When you pass through the waters,
>   I will be with you;
> and when you pass through the rivers,
>   they will not sweep over you.
> When you walk through the fire,
>   you will not be burned;
>   the flames will not set you ablaze...
> Since you are precious and honored in my sight
>   and because I love you...
> Do not be afraid, for I am with you.
> Isaiah 43:2, 4-5

13

Amazing!

Tim Hansel, in his book *You Gotta' Keep Dancing*, says:

> Joy has so much to do with how we see and hear and experience the world. It is not to be grasped, but to give away. It is not to be contained, but shared. Joy has more to do with who we are than what we have, more to do with the healthiness of our attitude than with the health of our body. Joy, above all else, is a selfless quality which is magnified when it is shared and minimized when it is selfishly grasped.[2]

He then tells a familiar story:

> There were once two men, both seriously ill, in the same small room of a great hospital. Quite a small room, just large enough for the pair of them—two beds, two bedside lockers, a door opening on the hall, and one window looking out on the world.
>
> One of the men, as part of his treatments, was allowed to sit up in bed for an hour in the afternoon, and his bed was next to the window.
>
> But the other man had to spend all his time flat on his back—and both of them had to be kept quiet and still. This was the reason they were in the small room by themselves, and they were grateful for peace and privacy—none of the bustle and clatter and prying eyes of the general ward for them.
>
> Of course, one of the disadvantages of their condition was that they weren't allowed to do much; no reading, no radio, certainly no television—they had to keep quiet and still, just the two of them.
>
> They used to talk for hours and hours—about their wives, their children, their homes, their jobs, their hobbies, their childhood, what they did during the war, where they'd been on vacation—all that sort of thing.
>
> Every afternoon, when the man in the bed next to the window was propped up for his hour, he would

pass the time by describing what he could see outside. The other man began to live for those hours.

The window apparently overlooked a park. There was a lake filled with ducks and swans, children throwing them bread and sailing model boats, and young lovers walking hand in hand beneath the trees. There were flowers and stretches of grass, games of softball, people taking their ease in the sunshine, and right at the back, behind the fringe of trees, a fine view of the city skyline.

The man on his back would listen to all of this, enjoying every minute—how a child nearly fell into the lake, how beautiful the girls were in their summer dresses, then an exciting ball game, or a boy playing with his puppy. It got to the place that he could almost see what was happening outside.

Then, one fine afternoon, when there was some sort of parade, the thought struck him: Why should the man next to the window have all the pleasure of seeing what was going on? Why shouldn't he get the chance?

He felt ashamed and tried not to think like that, but the more he tried, the worse he wanted a change. He'd do anything!

In a few days, he had turned sour. He should be by the window! He brooded, couldn't sleep, and grew even more seriously ill—which none of the doctors understood.

One night as he stared at the ceiling, the other man suddenly woke up, coughing and choking, the fluid congesting in his lungs, his hands groping for the button that would bring the night nurse running. But the man watched without moving.

The coughing racked the darkness—on and on—choked off—then stopped—the sound of breathing stopped—and the man continued to stare at the ceiling.

In the morning the day nurse came in with water for their baths and found the other man dead. They took away his body, quietly, no fuss.

As soon as it seemed decent, the man asked if he could be moved to the bed next to the window. They moved him, tucked him in, made him quite comfortable, and left him alone to be quiet and still.

The minute they'd gone, he propped himself up on one elbow, painfully and laboriously, and looked out the window.

It faced a blank wall.[3]

I'd like to be like the first man. I'd like to choose to introduce joy into the difficult situations of life—and make it come alive for those around me!

Whatever it is that is turning you from the little everyday miracles of living—whatever is keeping you from getting excited about the sacredness of each unrepeatable moment—I want you to recapture the miracle and regain a sense of awe and amazement at the intricate plans and promises of our mighty Maker and learn once again to find inspiration in the simple songs of life.

Scene by scene, chapter by chapter, let's discover how it all falls into place. It's a new beginning—a refreshing new song.

Questions

1. *What are some events in the seasons of life that might dull the senses and choke out the "wonder of it all"?*
2. *What is the attitude presented in Romans 5, 1 Peter 4:12, Psalm 51:12, and 2 Corinthians 1:24?*
3. *What is meant by "if you can't change the circumstances change the way you respond to them"?*
4. *How can a person with severe chronic pain experience joy?*
5. *What are some ways we "put off" joy?*
6. *Give some suggestions for one who is depressed and apathetic in their daily walk—with his/her mate, children, or spiritual walk.*
7. *What does Jesus remind us of concerning trouble in Matthew 6:33?*
8. *Read Psalm 23:1 in every version possible. Discuss the possibilities inherent in God as the Shepherd.*

9. Are there dangers in routine without diversity? In our daily walk? In congregational worship? In private worship?
10. Discuss the miracle of laughter and its healing effects (Prov. 23:1).

Chapter 2

I Stand Amazed...
at God, the Father

Imagine yourself standing at the foot of Mt. McKinley, the tallest peak in North America. You gaze upward, marveling at the overwhelming loveliness and stark grandeur of the massive, snow-covered peaks. All of a sudden a violent storm unleashes its fury. You can barely see the shape of the mountain through the curtain of dark, ominous clouds and thick, black smoke billowing from the top. Then, the mountain begins to rumble and shake, and above the tumultuous roar you hear the sound of a trumpet. It grows louder and louder until not even covering your ears can block out the shrill blasts. A loud voice appears out of nowhere, speaking words that cause you to tremble uncontrollably, for the voice warns that if you touch the mountain, you will die.

It seems like a scenario from the eruption of Mt. Saint Helens in the state of Washington, but it actually occurred in Moses' time. The place was Mt. Sinai, just before Moses was to receive the Ten Commandments (Ex. 10:16-20, Heb. 12:18-20). It was staged by God, the Father. He wanted to get the attention of the Israelites—to make them realize that He was all powerful—and this recording is but one of many that reveal His nature throughout Scripture.

Isaiah, the prophet, observed the living God, and what he saw and heard was so awesome that it marked the rest of his life. After his encounter, his special title for God became "the Holy One of Israel."

> In the year that King Uzziah died, I saw the Lord, seated on a throne, high and exalted, and the train of his robe filled the temple. Above him were seraphs, each with six wings: With two wings they covered their faces, with two they covered their feet, and with two they were flying. And they were calling to one another:
> "Holy, holy, holy is the Lord Almighty; the whole earth is full of His glory."
> At the sound of their voices, the posts and thresholds shook and the temple was filled with smoke.
> Isaiah 6:1-4

Nebuchadnezzar, an ancient king of Babylon, was an olden-days version of Saddam Hussein. An ego-maniac, he strutted proudly on the roof of the royal palace in Babylon, boasting that he was all-powerful and majestic.

God intervened, took away his authority, and banished him to the fields, where he became as a wild beast with claws like a bird and feathers of an eagle. There he was to remain, a mindless beast, until he acknowledged that God was the sovereign ruler of all the kingdoms of men and could give control of them to anyone of His choosing (Dan. 4:28-33).

At the end of his time in the fields, Nebuchadnezzar's sanity was restored, and he began to praise God, rather than himself:

> Now I, Nebuchadnezzar, praise and exalt and glorify the King of heaven, because everything he does is right and all his ways are just. And those who walk in pride he is able to humble.
> Daniel 4:37

Our encounters with God aren't quite so dramatic. Until we meet Him in heaven, we walk in faith and form our own image of His being.

God, a Personal Image

As a child, I visualized God as an old man with a long, flowing white robe and white hair, holding a big staff. I longed to see Him face-to-face, to reach out and touch Him, to feel His visible presence. In prayers, I pleaded with Him to appear for just a short moment in the dark stillness of my bedroom. I assured Him that our meeting would be totally secret!

Is your present image of God much the same as the one you held close in childhood, or has it undergone a significant transformation in past years? Several women, when asked to describe their visual conception of God, offered these descriptions:

> "I picture God as a very, very big man—almost like a giant. He has a very long white beard with piercing eyes, and there are little angels everywhere with harps. He sits in a seat that looks like a judge's seat in a courtroom. There are clouds everywhere. He has a very big book on His desk with a big feather pen."

> "I see a vague figure of God with His raiment of white flowing in the breeze. As I talk, the angels listen compassionately. When I've asked for forgiveness, shouts of glory rise from heaven..."

> "I picture God sitting in a field of green grass with a stream running through it and animals sitting beside Him as He listens to my prayers."

> "He is a bright light that always smiles."

J. B. Phillips wrote a book entitled *Your God is Too Small.* The thesis of the book is this: although our horizons have expanded, our concept of God remains almost virtually the same as it did in childhood. We are still attempting to worship the God of Sunday school years! Because our present-day capabilities are almost limitless, it's hard to imagine a God who can far exceed anything going on in the world today.

Phillips lists several inadequate conceptions of God:

1. **God is a very old gentleman who lives in heaven.** He is often pictured standing tall with a staff in His hands, with cheeks puffed out to visualize His control over the winds and weather. One child, when asked to draw a picture of God, drew a picture of a very old man sitting at a big switchboard, with switches labeled "thunder," "lightning," "rain," etc.

2. **The idea of God is hardly more than parental carry-over.** In other words, our parents take care of us until we get to a certain age, then God takes over. We respect Him, but no more than we respect our parents. We love Him, but no more than the love we have for our parents.

3. **God is the conscience.** He knows our every move and directs us to make important decisions between right and wrong.

4. **God is an escape from the troubles of the world.** To a non-Christian, God is psychological escapism! He is somewhere, someplace we can run and hide when life gets tough.

5. **God is a secondhand God.** The person who feels this is one who has never experienced first-hand the love and guidance of our Father. He has been told by others of His goodness.[1]

All of these conceptions are true to a certain degree. God DOES reign over earth, and He has set in motion the laws of nature which bring springtime and summer, hail and snow, sunshine and shadow. We love Him as a child loves a parent. He directs our path. He IS a refuge in the time of storm. We learn much of Him from others. However, none of these, standing alone, provide a total picture of the vastness of God's greatness, for the mystery surrounding Him is the most complex of all time. I cannot fathom His glory. God planned it that way.

> Oh, the depth of the riches of the wisdom and the knowledge of God! How unsearchable his judgments, and his paths beyond tracing out!
> Romans 11:33

Godly Words

The following are some words we often hear associated with God:

SOVEREIGN: God has the Divine Right to do as He chooses, for He never has to answer to anyone. He is never puzzled nor disturbed at events, for His purposes are always accomplished. Nothing is ever done without His permission or apart from His purpose.

OMNIPOTENT: God has the power and ability to do anything He chooses. Nothing is impossible. The creation and the resurrection are but two of the many occasions in which God showed His omnipotence.

> He who forms the mountains, creates the wind, and reveals his thoughts to man, he who turns dawn to darkness and treads the high places of the earth—the Lord God Almighty is his name.
>
> Amos 4:13

> For nothing is impossible with God.
>
> Luke 1:37

MAJESTIC:

> The Lord reigns, he is robed in majesty. The Lord is robed in majesty and is armed with strength. The world is firmly established; it cannot be moved. Your throne was established long ago; you are from all eternity. The seas have lifted up, O Lord, the seas have lifted up their voice; the seas have lifted up their pounding waves. Mightier than the thunder of the great waters, mightier than the breakers of the sea—the Lord on high is mighty. Your statutes stand firm; holiness adorns your house for endless days, O Lord.
>
> Psalm 93:1-5

These words point to the splendor and glory of God. In the temple and tabernacle a bright light usually accompanied the voice of the Lord. It was mysterious and blinding and filled the people with awe and reverence for God. Paul tells us that God "dwells in inapproachable light." In His presence we would fall

23

on bended knee in reverence and awe, much like an earthly subject falls to the ground in honor of a royal king or queen.

OMNISCIENT: His is the "all-seeing" eye. His knowledge is eternal, infinite, and limitless. He knows everything—past, present, and future. He touches us every moment. I feel as did the Psalmist in chapter 139 verse 6: "Such knowledge is too wonderful for me!"

OMNIPRESENT: His presence is universal, filling the heavens and the earth. He is very much aware of everything that transpires upon this planet and in the lives of His people.

JUST: As an honorable judge, God is just, righteous and totally impartial in His dealings with man—either in approving and rewarding, or in condemning and judging.

> Righteousness and justice are the foundation of your throne. Love and faithfulness go before you.
> Psalm 89:14

God describes Himself as just in Jeremiah 9:24:

> I am the Lord who exercises kindness, justice and righteousness on earth, for in these I delight.

HOLY: God operates in the realm of absolute perfection. He is totally incapable of evil.

> For all have sinned and fall short of the glory of God.
> Romans 3:23

The Hebrew word for "Holy" expresses the thought of something being "separated." God was separate in the sense that He was high above His creation. God told Isaiah,

> I live in a high and holy place.
> Isaiah 57:15

TRANSCENDENT: Man is a tiny speck in the universe, sharing it with tens of thousands of planets we can't even see. Scientists have discovered an infinite number of galaxies. God is over all and above all!

Christ, the Revelation of God

God sent Christ to the earth so that we might know, in our finite way, what He is like (John 1:1-4, 14). We can know how He lived, what He did, even what He thought. In everything He was the revelation of the nature of God. He is vast, unmeasured, boundless. He is under me, and around me, and before me. His love never fails.

> Who shall separate us from the love of Christ? Shall hardship or persecution or famine or nakedness or danger or sword?...No, in all these things we are more than conquerors through him who loves us. For I am convinced that...neither height nor depth, nor anything else in all creation, will be able to separate us from the love of God that is in Christ Jesus our Lord.
>
> Romans 8:35, 37-39

Robert Browning expressed it like this:

> If I forget,
>> Yet God remembers! If these hands of mine
> Cease from their clinging, yet the hands divine
>> Hold me so firmly that I cannot fall;
> And if sometimes I am too tired to call
>> For Him to help me, then He reads the prayer
> Unspoken in my heart, and lifts my care.
>
> I dare not fear, since certainly I know
>> That I am in God's keeping, shielded so
> From all that else would harm, and in the hour
>> Of stern temptation strengthened by His power;
> I tread no path in life to Him unknown;
>> I lift no burden, bear no pain, alone:
> My soul a calm, sure hiding-place has found:
>> The everlasting arms my life surrounds.
>
> God, Thou art love! I build my faith on that.
> I know Thee who has kept my path, and made
> Light for me in the darkness, tempering sorrow

So that it reached me like a solemn joy;
If it were too strange that I should doubt Thy Love.

Our Response to God

Knowing this God who defies description, who is over and above all that we can comprehend, should be life's major pursuit. As in any worthy endeavor, man must put forth some effort to once again capture the wonder and awe of the Father and to get to know Him better.

Get in the praise habit. Often we forget that our God is worthy of our praise as well as our problems! In fact, He delights in it! We should live in a continual spirit of thanksgiving.

We should praise Him for His greatness, for He cares for us and guides us faithfully all through life. He is interested in our days. His love for us is beyond comprehension!

O for a thousand tongues to sing
My great Redeemer's praise,
The glories of my God and King,
The triumphs of His grace!

My gracious Master and my God,
Assist me to proclaim,
To spread through all the earth abroad
The honors of Thy name!
—Hymn by Charles Wesley

Let everyone that has breath praise the Lord.
Psalm 150:6

Be still! Before you begin public or private worship, pause and think only of God. Try to visualize Him. Imagine yourself kneeling in His presence. Don't try to hurry through your devotion time. Don't think that you always have to be praying during your quiet time. Stop, be still, and simply think of God.

Be still, and know that I am God.
Psalm 46:10

Read daily from the Psalms. Use the Psalms as prayer. Make a notebook of verses pertaining to God. Keep it handy for times when you are having difficulty drawing near to Him.

The better you get to know your God, the more comfortable you will be with a loving, continual feast of praise and thanksgiving offered up to Him. Get to know Him as your rock, your fortress, your deliverer. Experience His vast, unmeasured, boundless love. Then, and only then, will you be able to live the "abundant" life in Christ Jesus.

Questions

1. *List ten adjectives describing God, the Father.*
2. *Look up the following verses and fill in the blanks with a word or phrase from each passage that describes God:*

   Isaiah 5:16 _____

   Isaiah 6:3 _____

   1 Corinthians 13 _____

   John 3:16 _____

3. *Through the years, many have replaced the "Thee" of prayers to "You." Discuss both sides of this issue.*
4. *Share with the class the times in which you have felt the closest to God and the farthest away.*
5. *How do we reconcile God's love with suffering?*
6. *What is the best way to teach the love of God to children? Is there a wrong way?*
7. *Share your childhood image of God.*
8. *Was the victory over the dictatorship of Saddam Hussein a victory of God, or a victory of man?*
9. *Exactly how much does God intervene in the affairs of man?*
10. *Discuss the attributes of God as found in Psalm 139. Read this Psalm aloud daily for the next week.*

Chapter 3

I Stand Amazed. . .
at the Glory of the Creation

Several years ago I had the privilege of spending a few days at the beach. The sound of the gentle pounding of the waves against the shore left in my heart forever the eternal song of the sea. On some days they were like a gentle caress—on others, a booming crash upon the sands. Their sounds were like a symphony of melodies played upon the waves, written and directed by the celestial music maker, God Himself.

Time and time again there stole over me an acute, undeniable awareness of the splendor and majesty of God. His artistry was exquisite. Yet this was but a fragment of the touch of His hand upon His creation!

> He gathers the waters of the sea into jars; he puts
> the deep into storehouses.
> Psalm 33:7

One night we lay on our backs in the sand and watched in breathless awe and wonderment as wave after wave of stars burst out of a darkening sky and sped downward across the horizon. The symphony continued with the sound of the waves added to the dazzling display of shooting stars.

God, or Man?

I wondered over and over how any sincere, honest, open-minded man could help but admit that it is not mere chance that caused the interaction of stars, the sun and moon, the oceans and tides, surf and sand. How could any competent, intelligent being embrace the theories of man rather than the statement of God concerning the creation?

Are there really those who would believe that we are but bare fragments of materials, shifted about on the planet in simple response to the forces around us? Could a mere human plan a universe with such precision and accuracy that the exact spot where two spaceships will meet in outer space can be calculated?

Did the world come into existence and maintain that existence through time and chance alone? Is it mere chance that creates a gravitational pull that will lift ten billion tons of water ten feet on a rising tide and cause it to come crashing down on the beaches of the world?

Those who support the "Big Bang" theory of the evolution of the earth hold the belief that many eons ago, two planets collided. One fragment drifted far enough from the sun that it began to cool. Condensation gathered, thus forming the oceans. Microscopic beings in the water began to develop and throughout the passage of time became more and more complex, eventually evolving into the complicated creature better known as "man."

Ezra, the prophet, gives a different interpretation of the beginning of life on Planet Earth:

> You alone are the Lord. You made the heavens,
> even the highest heavens, and all their starry host,
> the earth and all that is on it, the seas and all that
> is in them. You give life to everything, and the
> multitudes of heaven worship you.
>
> Nehemiah 9:6

Francis Schaeffer, author and theologian, believes that if the world was created from nothing but a piece of rock drifting in the universe, it would be an impersonal universe.[1] But God, an infinite Person, made man in His own image. He created a "people-oriented universe," complete with potential artists, poets, musicians, landscape gardeners, writers, etc. Our Maker created us in such a way that we can look at the universe and all that is contained therein and see that He is there and that He is a personal God.

The heavens are constantly declaring the glory of the Creator! The whole of creation communicates the wonder of who He is. The stars and moon testify that He exists, that He is the Supreme Artist!

> For since the creation of the world God's invisible qualities—his eternal power and divine nature—have been clearly seen, being understood from what has been made, so that men are without excuse.
>
> Romans 1:20

The Lord Himself explained it in simple terms to Job:

> Where were you when I laid the earth's foundation? Tell me, if you understand. Who marked off its dimensions? Surely you know! Who stretched a measuring line across it? On what were its footings set, or who laid its cornerstone while the morning stars sang together and all the angels shouted for joy? Who shut up the sea behind doors when it burst forth from the womb, when I made the clouds its garment and wrapped it in thick darkness...Have you ever given orders to the morning, or shown the dawn its place, that it might take the earth by the edges and shake the wicked out of it? The earth takes shape like clay under a seal; its features stand out like those of a garment.
>
> Job 38:4-9, 12-14

The Wonder of It All

Even if I were not a Christian and did not believe in God, the Creator, my aesthetic nature is such that I would have to argue that nothing less than a Supreme Being could create this beautiful earth. The magnificence of nature is an intricate part of my life, communicating in joyful song the glory of the Creator-God. I seek strength and endurance in places where great and elemental things prevail. There I can completely forget myself and become completely and totally immersed in the beauty of my surroundings.

A sense of smallness and insignificance, praise and honor, joy, exhilaration and inspiration flood my being in the presence of the Creation—whether it's on a mountain peak witnessing new vistas, rambling on a remote wooded path in the forest, viewing a sky aflame at sunset, or simply gazing upon the star-studded heavens on a clear evening. I am awed, humbled, and stilled, and the beauty which surrounds me sweeps my spirit with an overwhelming sense of gratitude—an indelible, irrefutable impression that "this is my Father's world." John Keats, the famous poet, wrote, "The poetry of earth is never dead."

I can visualize David, as he stood wonderstruck at the numberless stars of the deepest night, praising His creator in exquisite language in Psalm 19:1-2:

> The skies proclaim the work of his hands. Day after day they pour forth speech; night after night they display knowledge.

> When I consider your heavens, the work of your fingers, the moon and the stars, which you have set in place, what is man that you are mindful of him...
> O Lord, our Lord, how majestic is your name in all the earth!
> > Psalm 8:3-4, 9

How often we cast aside what we know about our Creator and His universe as we become choked in the chaos of the world in which we live. Our perceptions become dulled; our eyes do not see, our ears do not hear. How often I have glanced at the first rose of summer and forgotten to consider that in spite of all the time-consuming labor I put into making the rosebush grow and produce, it is still simply and utterly a miracle of the creation of God.

As a true Artist, God expresses deep satisfaction in what He has made. After He completed His creation, He "saw all that he had made, and it was very good (Gen. 1:31)." Can I do less?

For the beauty around me, for the strength it offers, for the peace it brings, I am thankful!

To have our spirits reborn we must break through the wall of insulation and see, touch, and feel the seasons and the beauties of nature: the lacework of winter, the scents of spring, the scorching warmth of a summer breeze, the climates, the wind and the weather. All are expressions of God. All have a vital message for our lives.

We must become as a little child, who sees wonder in even the smallest of God's creation. To see everything as if it were the first time—or perhaps the last—is to have the sensitivity of our spirit reborn.

Keepers of the Earth

Today there is a renewed interest in the Native American. Part of their culture was a sensitivity and appreciation of nature. They felt the earth was their Mother; the sky, their Father. Therefore, they could do it no harm. They knew nothing of our God, yet their entire life was enmeshed with worship for the creation. Each morning, before dawn, they went to a designated place and greeted the day with chants and prayers of thanksgiving. Some tribes placed their tepees so that the opening was toward the rising sun, so that they might worship immediately upon awakening.

We have much to learn from their example. Could we not greet each day with praise and thanksgiving? Could we not take better care of earth and all that is contained thereon?

Just a few decades ago, earth was losing about one species of plant life a year. That now occurs every day. Environmental leaders worldwide plead for efforts to save the Brazilian rain forest, yet many of their pleas fall on deaf ears. Last year alone an area larger than Great Britain fell to chain saws. Fifty acres a second are destroyed worldwide.

I reason deep within myself that I have a holy obligation to protect and preserve what God has given me, and to fulfill that obligation I teach environmental issues to the children in my class each year. However, long before I approach a study on animals of the world, pollution, or the "greenhouse effect," I attempt to teach them to love and appreciate the world and to be humbly in sympathy with all the creatures that dwell here.

I teach them to use all their senses when outdoors—to open their eyes and ears and listen to nature. One day we might be found hugging a tree; another, inspecting tiny insects in the grass with a looking glass. We continually remind ourselves and others of the beauty of the creation. Why? Because we will only respect and care for something we love. Love for earth can only come through experiencing it with all our senses.

Nature Study—A Mini-Course

In order to deepen your own aesthetic appreciation of God's creation, allow me to make several suggestions taken from my own experiences:

1. Read at least one Psalm per day pertaining to Creation.

2. Try to spend at least thirty minutes outdoors each day. Feel the essence of life in nature. Turn away for a short while and absorb the beauty of the Creation. Visit natural areas—parks, forests, wildlife preserves, etc.

3. Become like a child. Take a little one for a walk. Share in their sense of wonder and discovery as they experience each moment in nature with awe and delight.

4. Become an active environmentalist. Keep up with issues concerning the preservation of nature. Recycle. Conserve energy.

5. Begin a library of nature books and videos. Use art as a channel for God to speak to you through His divine work.

6. Take an interest in photography. Keep a scrapbook of beautiful places in nature.

7. Keep a sketch pad handy. (And make sure that your child has art supplies available!)

8. Continue daily in prayers of thanksgiving for the lovely things of nature.

How appropriate to pray at the beginning of each day:

"Thank you, God, for this earth, our home; for the wide sky and the blessed sun, for the salt sea and the running water, for the everlasting hills and the never-resting winds, for trees and the common grass underfoot. We thank you for our senses by which we hear the songs of birds, and see the splendor of the summer fields, and taste of the autumn fruits, and rejoice in the feel of the snow, and smell the breath of the spring. Grant us a heart wide-open to all this beauty; and save our souls from being so blind that we pass unseeing when even the common thornbush is aflame with your glory, O God our creator, who lives and reigns for ever and ever."[2]

Some say God is found only in elaborate houses of worship. I believe He softly meets the soul in the amphitheater of His Creation.

Questions

1. *Read the following verses in Job 38, and write the questions God asked Job concerning His creation of the world.*

   *Vs. 16*_____

   *Vs. 17*_____

   *Vs. 18*_____

   *Vs. 19*_____

   *Vs. 20*_____

   *Vs. 22*_____

   *Vs. 24*_____

   *Vs. 25*_____

   *Vs. 28*_____

   Vs. 29-30 _____

2. *Read the remaining verses in this chapter and in chapter 39 and meditate on the majesty of God and the insignificance of man.*

3. Read Psalm 8 and discuss the responsibility God has placed on man to take care of the earth. In what ways have we failed?
4. In Genesis 1, how many times do you find the words "after their kind"? What is the significance of this?
5. Does 1 Corinthians 15:39 convey the same idea? Discuss.
6. Ask a young child about the creation of the world. Write down his observations and questions and share with the class.
7. Using the following chapters and verses, discuss God's provision for man through nature.
   Genesis 1
   Deuteronomy 28
   Psalm 104
   Luke 12
8. What do the inspired writers of Scripture have to say about the Creation?
   Psalm 24
   Isaiah 48
   Acts 4
   Romans 1:20
9. Discuss current environmental issues.

Chapter 4

I Stand Amazed...
at the Promises of God

Just last week our one and only daughter became a wife. During the wedding ceremony I listened carefully to the vows which she and John had written. They promised to nurture and support one another, to allow the other to experience growth and freedom, to take care of each other in both the good and bad times.

Our very lives are dependent on the promises made by others and the faithful fulfillment of those promises, from the bride or groom who promises to stand by our side forever, the weatherman, the repairman, the butcher and baker to the insurance company which protects us. We implicitly trust the promises of politicians and will "swallow" anything presented by the advertising industry. Unfortunately, most do not view their promise as a sacred trust, and many leave grief, pain, sorrow, and anger in their wake.

Last spring we had a leak in our roof. For weeks we called a roofing man almost daily and pleaded for him to repair the roof. His promise was always, "I'll be there first thing tomorrow." Day after day, week after week, we waited. The scenario was repeated several times until finally, after six weeks, we found a roofer who kept his promise.

In preparation for our daughter's wedding, we had to write a LOT of checks. There was the florist, the musician, the caterer, etc. Because we were paying for the majority of wedding expenses, we would often give Terri a check bearing our signature to cover the cost of the services needed.

We would have felt very badly if Terri had torn up our checks and said, "Mom and Dad never keep their promises. They don't have enough money in the bank to pay for this wedding. This is just a useless scrap of paper!"

God, the Holy and Infinite Father, has left us promises on a scrap of paper—definite promises that are meant to be believed. Promises that will take care of us until He returns. They are "blank checks," to be used repeatedly in any situation, and the more they're used with faith, the more powerful they become![1]

For example:

Pay to the order of _____
"And whatsoever you ask in my name, that will I do..."
John 14:13

Pay to the order of _____
"Whatever you ask for in prayer, believe that you have received it, and it will be yours."
Mark 11:24

Amazing! God makes a promise—and He keeps it! Throughout Scripture are recorded promise after promise made by God. All have already been fulfilled or remain to be fulfilled. And God has full intention of seeing them through!

Nature And Purpose Of Promises

HIS PROMISES ARE PRECIOUS AND EXCEEDING GREAT!
Scripture records 32,000 promises regarding salvation, strength for daily burdens, heaven, and the Christian walk.

> Through these he has given us his very great and
> precious promises, so that through them you may
> participate in the divine nature and escape the
> corruption in the world caused by evil desires.
> 2 Peter 1:4

Note the usage of the adjectives "great" and "precious." New Testament writers wrote in journalistic style. Their speech was free of flowery adjectives and descriptive words. Even the record of the phenomenal happenings of Pentecost is remarkably precise. The inclusion of these adjectives points to the remarkable nature and scope of these promises and emphasizes that His promises **are** great in number, and extremely precious!

I found out just recently how manifold ARE those promises. I began a notebook and attempted to write down every promise I found in the Scripture. I filled page after page through the weeks, but soon realized the enormous impossibility of the task. Instead, I began to underline those promises in Scripture and place beside them a "P." It is truly inspiring to be constantly reminded of the thousands of beautiful promises that are mine throughout Scripture!

HIS PROMISES STRENGTHEN OUR FAITH

Abraham's faith was strengthened through the knowledge of God's promise. Though one hundred years old and his wife barren, he still believed that he would become the father of many nations, as had been promised to him:

> Yet he did not waver through unbelief regarding the promise of God, but was strengthened in his faith and gave glory to God, being fully persuaded that God had power to do what he had promised.
> Romans 4:20

Pay close attention to the words "being fully persuaded." There aren't too many things in this life of which I am "fully persuaded." Even simple decisions are difficult. Never am I fully persuaded as to which candidate to vote for in an election. I'm never certain which diet to try next. I even have trouble picking a brand of toothpaste!

Children are different. Once they believe in something, they give it their whole heart. In their early childhood, my children were "fully persuaded" that Ken and I had unlimited power. They later transferred that feeling of awe to their teachers. Hopefully, they have reached adulthood with a sure, unwavering certainty of the blessings which result from a walk with Christ.

God has given us His promises. Now it's up to us to be like Abraham, never wavering through unbelief, but knowing that our amazing God has the power to do what He has promised.

HIS PROMISES KEEP US PURE IN OUR DAILY WALK

> Since we have these promises, dear friends, let us purify ourselves from everything that contaminates body and spirit, perfecting holiness out of reverence for God.
>
> 2 Corinthians 7:1

I could make some major changes in this verse and write it on the board for my students the first day of school:

> Dear students: I promise you this. If you do good work, you will get good grades! Since you have this promise, get to work! Clear your mind of anything that inhibits the learning process, and work on perfecting your study habits! If you do these things, then good grades will follow.

Anytime I am guaranteed a reward after a particular effort, I am more prone to give of myself. As Christians, we are told in the verse from 2 Corinthians to purify ourselves because we have "the promises." Because I have a promise of eternity waiting for me at the end of this life, I will make every attempt to live in purity and obedience to His will, striving for the perfection which He desires. Then, His beautiful promise of eternal life will be fulfilled:

> But we know that when he appears, we shall be like him, for we shall see him as he is. Everyone who has this hope in him purifies himself, just as he is pure.
>
> 1 John 3:2-3

To see Him—after waiting all these years! To be able to look into His eyes and see the love which has flowed for His children down through the eons of time! To be able to touch the hem of His garment! To walk with Him in the cool shade of evening! To be like Him! To be transformed in the twinkling of an eye to His likeness! That one precious promise is enough to keep me strong and pure on this earthly walk.

HIS PROMISES ARE CERTAIN OF FULFILLMENT

> For no matter how many promises God has made, they are "Yes" in Christ. And so through him the "Amen" is spoken by us to the glory of God.
> 2 Corinthians 1:20

I have to admit—I don't put a lot of stock in "people" promises. Because of the uncertainty of life, the nature of the world, and the unstable circumstances which surround us, promises can't always be fulfilled to our heart's desire.

My husband can promise me a trip to Alaska for our twenty-fifth anniversary next summer, but I know that the promise is contingent on family and financial circumstances at the time. I can promise my publisher that I will have two chapters of this book ready by next Friday, but something unforeseen can happen to delay the deadline.

God's promises aren't contingent on human circumstances! He can make as many as He chooses, and we can know that each of them will come to be. Even the Old Testament bears witness of the absolute integrity of God's promises:

> Know therefore that the Lord your God is God; he is the faithful God, keeping his covenant of love to a thousand generations of those who love him and keep his commands.
> Deuteronomy 7:9

> You know with all your heart and soul that not one of all the good promises the Lord your God gave you has failed. Every promise has been fulfilled; not one has failed.
> Joshua 23:14

41

God is not a man, that he should lie, nor a son of man that he should change his mind. Does he speak and then not act? Does he promise and not fulfill?

Numbers 23:19

There's a banquet in the pages of Scripture of the permanent and enduring promises of our God. Promises to Adam and Eve; to Noah, Abraham and Lot; to the city of Babylon; and to the church today. Promise after promise has come to fulfillment.
Amazing!

A Look At Some Special Promises

YOU'LL NEVER WALK ALONE

So do not fear, for I am with you; do not be dismayed, for I am your God. I will strengthen you and help you; I will uphold you with my righteous right hand.

Isaiah 41:10

A preacher once told a story that took place in the pioneer days of our country:

There was a young boy who had to walk to school each day through a dense forest. He lived in mortal fear of running into a bear or wild Indians in the backwoods. Often he begged his father to let him stay home, but his father wanted him to learn to be brave, so he sent him on his way with a pat on his back and a word of encouragement.
Gradually, the boy's fears subsided.
Then, one day, as he entered the forest, he stood face-to-face with a big brown grizzly bear. Paralyzed with fear, he knew death was imminent. As he stood, trembling, a shot rang out. The bear fell dead. Out of the bushes stepped his father, rifle in hand.

"It's alright, son. Every day I have followed you to school, and have been waiting for you each afternoon. I was always ready to protect you. But I didn't want you to see me—for I wanted you to learn to be brave."

God promised His children that He would always go with them, just as the father went with his son. We can't visibly sense His presence, but He is always there, ready to protect us from harm.

3,400 years ago God promised Joshua that if he moved himself and two million others across the Jordan that He would give him all the land promised to his people.

I will give you every place where you set your foot.
Joshua 1:3

Joshua stepped out in quiet faith, right into the Jordan, and God held back the river. He flattened the walls of Jericho and Joshua marched around it.

Amazing!

He's with us, even though sometimes we, too, must walk in the shadows of the forest. He's there—when the storms of life beat at our door and leave us whimpering in darkness. He's there—when the laws of nature wreak havoc on hearth and home.

When loved ones die, He is there. He sustains and upholds us and gives us strength through those He sends to help us through our pain. His presence enables us to surmount every sorrow, turmoil, stress and darkness. He brings comfort, consolation and renewal.

He never deserts us, just as He promised:

And surely I am with you always.
Matthew 28:20

My presence shall be with you,
Most blest assurance here;
While in this lower valley,
Beset by doubt and fear.
No evil shall befall thee,

Close sheltered to thy breast,
My presence shall go with thee,
And I will give thee rest.

Author unknown

NO NEED TO WORRY

And why do you worry about clothes? See how the lilies of the field grow. They do not labor or spin. Yet I tell you that not even Solomon in all his splendor was dressed like one of these. If that is how God clothes the grass of the field, which is here today and tomorrow is thrown into the fire, will he not much more clothe you, O you of little faith? So do not worry, saying "What shall we eat?" or "What shall we wear?" For the pagans run after all these things, and your heavenly father knows that you need them. But seek first his kingdom and his righteousness, and all these things will be given to you as well.

Matthew 6:28-33

In this passage from the Sermon on the Mount Jesus assured His apostles that God knew all their needs and that they had no reason to be anxious.

To be honest, I DO worry. I worry about college tuition, and groceries, and weddings, and the mortgage, and on and on. But worry for material possessions is NOT necessary in the Kingdom of God. Our Father takes care of His children! He does not forsake those who do His will!

My God will meet all your needs.

Philippians 4:19

David, the psalmist, said,

I was young and now I am old, yet I have never seen the righteous forsaken, or their children begging bread.

Psalm 37:25

WRAPPED IN WHITE

One of the most precious promises is the one that states that no matter how deep into the depths of sin, God will wash and make me clean. He will cover all my deficiencies, making me as white as the new-fallen snows of winter.

> "Come now, let us reason together," says the Lord. "Though your sins are like scarlet, they shall be as white as snow. Though they are red as crimson, they shall be like wool."
>
> Isaiah 1:18

He forgets our sins—forever.

> For I will forgive their wickedness and will remember their sins no more.
>
> Hebrews 8:12

His Son came to earth and died on the cross, opening the way to Eternity for all mankind.

> And this is what He promised us—even eternal life.
>
> 1 John 2:25

> And this is the testimony: God has given us eternal life, and this life is in his Son.
>
> 1 John 5:11

Amazing!

HE LEADS THE WAY

I stand amazed at God's direction in my life. From early childhood until the present, I have felt Him directing my path. He worked His will in my life through family, through other Christians, and through unusual circumstances. I could draw a footpath of stones labeled with events and people who were part of His unfolding plan for my life.

Why should I be surprised? It's a simple promise, fulfilled:

Trust in the Lord with all your heart and lean not on your own understanding; in all your ways acknowledge him, and he will make your paths straight.

Proverbs 3:5-6

Commit to the Lord whatever you do, and your plans will succeed.

Proverbs 16:3

God's promises are amazing! But they have the power to move men only according to the value placed upon them, and according to the faith they have in the One who made the promise. We have to ACCEPT the promises, in deep gratitude and humility!

Do you want to live eternally?   Believe the promise!
Do you want strength to bear your burdens? Believe!
Do you want guidance in your daily walk? Believe!

Standing on the promises of Christ my King,
Thru eternal ages let His praises ring;
Glory in the highest I will shout and sing,
Standing on the promises of God.

—R. Kelso Carter

Questions

1. *What was the greatest promise of God—made at the beginning of time (John 3:16)?*
2. *List ten promises made to the Israelites in the Old Testament.*

   (1) _____

   (2) _____

   (3) _____

   (4) _____

(5) _____

(6) _____

(7) _____

(8) _____

(9) _____

(10) _____

3. God has promised to forgive our sins if we are His children. What is the promise given in Micah 7:19 regarding this?
4. Some might perceive God to be slow concerning His promises. What are two reasons for this according to Numbers 23:19?
5. Name a time someone has broken a promise to you.
6. How adamant should we be about keeping our promises?
7. How can we best teach our children to keep a promise?
8. What is the difference in "conditional" and "unconditional" promises?
9. Name some unconditional promises found in:
   Genesis 8:22
   Acts 1:9-11
   John 5:28-29
10. Name some conditional promises found in:
   Acts 2:38
   1 John 1:7, 9
   Acts 5:32
   Galatians 4:6
   Romans 8:28
   Romans 8:11
   James 1:2
   Revelation 2:10
   What is the "condition" required for the fulfillment of these promises?

Chapter 5

I Stand Amazed...
at the Incarnation

Away in a manger, no crib for his bed,
The little Lord Jesus lay down his sweet head.
The stars in the sky look down where he lay,
The little Lord Jesus asleep in the hay.

The cattle are lowing, the baby awakes,
The little Lord Jesus, no crying He makes.
I love Thee, Lord Jesus! Look down from the sky,
And stay by my side until morning is nigh.
                                    —Anonymous

As I write this chapter, it's the holiday season. I've spent the last month surrounded by the sights, smells, and sounds of the season. Carols ring out the news of the birth of Christ, and although our holiday celebrations do not center on such, it is difficult to pass through the season without being reminded of this great event that changed the world. The famous carol written above repeatedly comes to mind as I think of that magnificent miracle when He who made all things came to this world as a babe, to lie as a helpless human infant, nestled in His mother's arms. The invisible, spiritual God became human.

The Word became flesh and made his dwelling
among us.
John 1:14

It's a dramatic saga—a story of angels, dreams, and a virgin
who conceives and bears a son. The story of the birth of Christ
is a story as filled with action as any prime time made-for-
television movie! It was not just another historical event meant
to be viewed through secondhand lenses. It's the story of a man
who set the world on fire and left it changed forever. Jesus
Christ, the Messiah...fascinating...solid...real. Born of God, He
was brought into this world not to live, but to die.

Involved in the birth was a magnificent cast of players, each
an order of God's creation:

> The star (nature)
> Foreign nationalities (the Magi) representing all
> ethnic groups
> Powerful leaders (Herod the Great)
> The wealth of earth (gifts of the Magi)
> The law (both Roman and Jewish)
> The priesthood (Zechariah)
> The poor of earth (shepherds)
> Animals
> The angels[1]

All of these elements were perfectly orchestrated by God—
perfectly planned, from beginning to end! Each detail points
to the fact that this was no spur-of-the-moment decision—no
accident—no coincidence. The birth had been foretold by the
prophets some six hundred years earlier:

> For to us a child is born,
> to us a child is given,
> and the government will be on his shoulders.
> And He will be called
> Wonderful Counselor, Mighty God,
> Everlasting Father, Prince of Peace.
> Isaiah 9:6

Therefore the Lord Himself will give you a sign:
The virgin will be with child and will give birth to a
son, and will call him Immanuel.
Isaiah 7:14

In the story of the birth, the virgin Mary conceives a child through the Holy Spirit. Joseph, her fiancé, learns the explanation for her pregnancy through a dream in which the Lord speaks to him:

But after he had considered this, an angel of the Lord appeared to him in a dream and said, "Joseph son of David, do not be afraid to take Mary home as your wife, because what is conceived in her is from the Holy Spirit. She will give birth to a son, and you are to give him the name Jesus, because he will save his people from their sins.
Matthew 1:20-21

What takes place after that amazing revelation is told in Luke 2:

Joseph went from the town of Nazareth, in Galilee, to Judea, to the town named Bethlehem, where King David was born...He went to register himself with Mary, who was promised in marriage to him. She was pregnant, and while they were in Bethlehem, the time came for her to have her baby. She gave birth to her first son, wrapped Him in cloths and laid Him in a manger—there was no room for them to stay in the inn.

The Scene in Bethlehem
Jesus, the prophesied Messiah, slipped in while the rest of the world was sleeping. Not in a famed city with great majesty and pomp, such as Rome. Not in a temple, where one might expect to find a royal birth occur. This one who was born as an equal with God—the agent of creation (Heb. 1:2) and the source of light and life (John 1:4-5)—entered this world in Bethlehem, a shepherds' village. Weary travelers thronged its

streets. It could be likened to a busy train depot, where people stop for a layover, rest, and then move on to the next train—the next departure.

There were no luxury hotels nearby. There was not even a small room where Mary could rest in comfort and bear this child who was to be the Savior of the world. Over and over Mary and Joseph were turned away as they tried to find lodging. They were footsore and weary from their long journey from the village of Nazareth, five miles on the other side of Jerusalem. Finally, they came to rest in the only place left—a stable—a place where shepherds sheltered their flocks in times of storm. Nearby was a feeding trough, possibly made of stone. It was a place of deprivation, the filthiest place in the world, a place of lonely abandonment. It most likely reeked of manure and urine that had accumulated through the years. The manger was covered with cobwebs and debris fallen from the rock ceiling. Not a likely place for the birth of a promised Messiah!

Fulton Sheen, in *Life of Christ*, describes it so aptly:

> No worldly mind would ever have suspected that He Who could make the sun warm the earth would one day have need of an ox and an ass to warm Him with their breath; that He Who, in the language of Scriptures, could stop the turning about of Arcturus would have His birthplace dictated by an imperial census; that He Who clothed the fields with grass, would Himself be naked; that He, from Whose hands came planets and worlds, would one day have tiny arms that were not long enough to touch the huge heads of the cattle; that the feet which trod the everlasting hills would one day be too weak to walk; that the Eternal Word would be dumb; that Omnipotence would be wrapped in swaddling clothes; that Salvation would lie in a manger; that the bird which built the nest would be hatched therein; no one would have ever suspected that God coming to this earth would ever be so helpless.[2]

Infant holy, infant lowly, for His bed a cattle stall; Oxen lowing, little knowing Christ, the babe is Lord of all.
(Polish carol)

Child in the manger, Infant of Mary,
Came as a stranger, born in the stall;
Sweet little Jesus sent down from heaven,
God's gift of new life offered to all.

(Gaelic melody)

This King of Kings was born of Mary, a Jewish maiden—betrothed at a young age, frightened, bewildered, and probably scorned by family and friends. A friend of mine who has traveled in Israel cites examples of Jewish girls who are sometimes killed by their brothers because of the disgrace of a pregnancy outside of marriage. Although we have no proof of such in the times of Christ, no doubt Mary had to deal with much of the same attitude. Yet she trusted completely in God and accepted with humble submission the announcement by the angel:

Do not be afraid, Mary, you have found favor with God. You will be with child and give birth to a son, and you are to give him the name Jesus. He will be great and will be called the Son of the Most High. The Lord God will give him the throne of his father David, and he will reign over the house of Jacob forever; his kingdom will never end.

The Holy Spirit will come upon you, and the power of the Most High will overshadow you. So the holy one to be born will be called the Son of God.

Luke 1:30-33, 35

And so it was. Can you not catch the wonder?

The Shepherds and Angels

One of the greatest joys of heaven will be a close association with angels, the messengers of God. Although our knowledge is limited, we know that they carried God's message to specially chosen individuals. Many of their appearances describe them praising God (Isa. 6:3).

Angels played a role of paramount importance in the birth of Christ. God sent them to the shepherds to tell of the special birth.

It was an ordinary night. The shepherds were dozing off and on, sleepily keeping their watch on the woolly little lambs.

53

Suddenly it was as bright as a noonday sun. A bright light flowing from heaven bathed the earth with a radiant, resplendent blinding glory. The shepherds were speechless with fear, until the voice of the angel spoke to them and stilled their fears.

And there were shepherds living out in the fields nearby, keeping watch over their flocks at night. An angel of the Lord appeared to them, and the glory of the Lord shone around them, and they were terrified. But the angel said to them, "Do not be afraid. I bring you good news of great joy that will be for all the people. Today in the town of David a Savior has been born to you; he is Christ the Lord. This will be a sign to you: You will find a baby wrapped in cloths and lying in a manger." Suddenly a great company of the heavenly host appeared with the angel, praising God and saying,
"Glory to God in the highest, and on earth peace to men on whom his favor rests."

Luke 2:8-14

The shepherds didn't linger! They immediately conferred and agreed to go to Bethlehem and seek out this babe who was born in a manger.

So they hurried off and found Mary and Joseph, and the baby, who was lying in the manger. When they had seen him, they spread the word concerning what had been told them about this child, and all who heard it were amazed at what the shepherds said to them.

Luke 2:16-18

Can you not feel the wonder?

Joy to the world! The Lord has come.
Let earth receive her King.
Let every heart prepare Him room,
And heaven and nature sing....

54

Joy to the world! The Savior reigns.
Let men their songs employ.
While fields and floods, rocks, hills, and plains
Repeat the sounding joy....

No more let sins and sorrows grow,
Nor thorns infest the ground;
He comes to make His blessings flow
Far as the curse is found!

He rules the world, with truth and grace.
And makes the nations prove
The glories of His righteousness,
And wonders of His love!

His birth was humble; His parents of low socio-economic status; His hometown insignificant; His name—a common one. He didn't come to be a military leader, a healer, a philosopher, or a great political figure. He came to die—to pay a price.

And the story continues...the Magi, led by a star to visit the Baby and bring Him gifts, an insecure king who murders all children under age two in hopes to rid his kingdom of a possible replacement, a narrow escape, a dangerous journey into exile, safety at last in Nazareth, and the Christ child as He grows into adulthood.

Jesus, the Child

While the birth of Jesus was marked by supernatural events, He had a perfectly normal childhood. God had sent Him into this world as a real human, to be raised as a normal child. We can't assume that Jesus was exempted from the experiences of the real life. We can't make Him into a fairy tale romantic figure who grew up in a magical land far from the difficult realities of life, including pain and temptation.

He probably had the usual childhood diseases, problems with His brothers and sisters, and with the neighborhood children. He, too, had to go through the agonies of growing up; and was, just as we, required to be in submission to His parents. We read of His passing from infancy to childhood, from childhood to youth, and from youth to manhood.

Raised in a Jewish home, His life centered on the Holy Scripture. It became His meat and drink, and it kindled a flame within that was never extinguished.

He was taught by His parents and in the synagogue school. The temple scholars were awed by His questions and conclusions, a sign of His deep commitment to a study and understanding of the Law.

Throughout His youth, God was uniquely active in His life. He grew both physically, intellectually, and spiritually.

> And the child grew and became strong; he was filled with wisdom, and the grace of God was upon him.
>
> Luke 2:40

He learned the trade of carpentry while He waited patiently, humbly, and obediently. Real-life experiences gave Him a deep insight into toughness, gentleness, sickness and poverty. At the age of thirty, He marked the close of His private life and the beginning of His public ministry through His baptism by John.

In Conclusion

It's 4:00 a.m., and as I close out this chapter in the hushed stillness of the early morning, I am renewed afresh at the wonder of this simple story. In past weeks I have surrounded myself with both written and spoken words on the Incarnation. I have relived the events from a new perspective. I have gained new insights into God's purpose for Christ and His ultimate purpose for my own life.

I must admit, the story of the birth had lost much of its ability to stir the heart. Apathy had crept in unawares, whispering in lifeless undertones to a lifeless spirit. In retelling the story, I have made it once again real, and it is doubtful that I will ever be the same again.

Each of us has to meet Jesus on our own terms and in our own places—whether it be in the writing of a book, the keeping of a journal, our personal devotional life, a brief encounter, or a detailed study. God, the Father, seems to know exactly what we need. If we but ask, He will work through art, music, the printed page or the spoken word to awaken afresh our love for Him.

In writing this lesson, I have necessarily left out many details that can be read about in the gospel accounts of the birth of Christ. I have attempted to include those events which speak to me with their simplicity and their magnificence.

What would it take to bring back the spark of wonder and awe at the story of Jesus, the babe? What would it take to make you take a deep breath and let the wonder of Jesus in just one more time? And then again, and again, until each time the amazement washes over you like a spring rain and leaves you breathless with awe.

Get amazed! Sense the wonder!

Questions
1. Describe Mary's visit to Elizabeth in Luke 1.
2. Mary totally accepted the news that she was to bear the Christ child. Share with the class any incidences in which you have been willing to accept embarrassing questions and ridicule from people to accomplish God's purpose for your life.
3. In what way can the shepherds' reaction to the news of the birth be an example to us in our evangelistic efforts?
4. How did God use His natural creation to achieve His redemptive purposes (Matt. 2:2, 9)?
5. What was the prophesy made in Isaiah 60:6 regarding the gifts of the Magi?
6. How did God use the dreams of angels to guide Joseph as he protected the baby from jealous politicians?
7. Jesus is called _____ in John 4:42, 1 John 4:14, Acts 5:31, and Acts 13:23.
8. How do Mary and Joseph illustrate a devotion to God essential for family life (Luke 2:41)?
9. Relate the incident in Luke 2:49 that showed Jesus' commitment to the Law and His knowledge of His position in life as the Redeemer of mankind.
10. How can our familiarity with the story of Christ's birth affect our appreciation and awe of the incarnation?

Chapter 6

I Stand Amazed...
at Jesus, the Messiah

Everyone loves the tender story of the birth of the Christ Child. But the birth of the Messiah is only a small part of the complete plan put into effect by God, the Father. Salvation doesn't come through a baby. It comes through an event which took place some thirty-three years later and changed the entire course of the world. And so we continue the story of Jesus Christ, Savior of mankind...

> Tell me the story of Jesus,
> Write on my heart every word.
> Tell me the story most precious,
> Sweetest that ever was heard.
> —Fanny J. Crosby

Jesus, the Master Teacher

Millions of followers watched in shock a prime-time news special last week which exposed the deception, fraud and deceit of several popular television evangelists. One by one they tried in vain to defend their actions, piling lie upon lie, digging the hole of guilt deeper and deeper.

What a contrast to the ministry of our Lord. Jesus never spoke on television. He never raised money nor wrote a book. He was not a media personality, nor did He ever speak in a huge cathedral or build a multi-million dollar house of worship. He never asked for anything, but instead gave everything away.

Unlike the vain pompousness of many ministers of the Word, He avoided drawing attention and praise to Himself. He didn't come to be a philosopher or healer. He preferred a quiet conversation with a few rather than the glamour of many.

His title of choice was "teacher," yet He never attended preaching school, or seminars on how to be effective. He didn't use bulletin boards, or computers, or VCR tapes to get His message across. He was a master in the use of unorthodox visual aids. His lesson illustrations came from nature, children, and the rural life.

He spoke in unusual places: a party, a boat, the side of a hill, a field, on the roadside, and by the side of a lake. Crowds clamored after Him and listened with delight to His words, always begging for more (Mark 11:18). When He spoke, He had the ability to hush a noisy crowd instantaneously. His message struck straight to the heart of the rich and the poor, the lame and the blind, those broken in heart and spirit, and those heavily burdened with sin. He made bold claims of forgiveness of sins and taught that God loves all—both sinners and the upright. The crowds were amazed at His teachings (Matt. 22:33).

Gordon McDonald, author of *Forging a Real-World Faith*, says of Him:

> The multi-faceted style of Jesus leaves me breathless with its simplicity, its directness, its ability to inflame the hearts of people to faith and change.[1]

Forging boldly through comfort zones to confront hypocrisy, He could change a life with just a few simple words. He taught love and compassion rather than rules and laws. His one burning desire was to inspire His listeners to share God's love by loving others—even their enemies. He centered His messages on a singular unorthodox theme: the Kingdom of God and our relationship to Him. He wanted His followers to experience the abundant life—a life of wholeness and peace.

This Jesus was indeed a "king," but not in the familiar sense of the word. His subjects did not serve Him out of terror or fear, for He chose to live as we do—to experience the pains and conflicts of life. Thus He was empowered to have a part in our suffering.

> For we do not have a high priest who is unable to sympathize with our weaknesses, but we have one who has been tempted in every way, just as we are—yet was without sin.
>
> Hebrews 4:15

Reasons for His Successful Ministry

Jesus spent thirty years establishing His credibility in the community. He was a common man before He began to act as the Messiah. Before He taught the people, He walked with them through Bethlehem, Judea, Egypt, Nazareth, and the desert. He loved the common man and chose His followers from the ordinary people of His time: fishermen, corrupt tax collectors, doubters, and cowards.

His was a ministry marked by dynamic signs (Matt. 12:38), parables, object lessons, and applications. It was also marked with endless distractions—helping a dying child, a blind man, a bleeding woman, a publican sitting in a tree, and a grieving family. Yet with His eyes forever locked on Calvary, He knew His singular purpose and goal. His steps never faltered. His purpose never varied.

And thus He walked the path to Calvary.

> For me it was in the garden,
> He prayed, "Not my will, but thine."
> He had no tears for His own grief,
> But sweatdrops of blood for mine.
>
> In pity angels beheld Him,
> And came from the world of light.
> To comfort Him in the sorrows
> He bore for my soul that night.
>
> He took my sins and my sorrows,
> He made them His very own.
> He bore the burden to Calvary,
> And suffered and died alone.
>
> —Charles H. Gabriel

61

I stand amazed...at

The Miracle of the Cross

> ...and the Lord Jesus Christ, who gave himself for
> our sins.
> > Galatians 1:3-4

> But God demonstrates his own love for us in this:
> While we were still sinners, Christ died for us.
> > Romans 5:8

> God made him who had no sin to be sin for us, so
> that in him we might become the righteousness of
> God.
> > 2 Corinthians 5:21

It's difficult to conceive in this day of isolationism and humanism why someone would demonstrate His love for me in such a way! Often as I view "911," the television program which reenacts heroic and unselfish rescue attempts, I think of the sacrifice of those who act without a second thought when they see someone in perilous trouble. Deep within all of us there seems to be an instantaneous reaction to come through in times of trouble—even if it might mean losing our own lives.

Our Lord was not forced. He was not coerced. He did not weep or thrash out against God, as so often we do. He knew the terrible price He was about to pay, yet His attitude was always, "Not my will, but thine."

In Hebrews 10:5-7, Jesus speaks to God of what is to come:

> Sacrifice and offering you did not desire, but a
> body you prepared for me; with burnt offerings and
> sin offerings you were not pleased. Then I said,
> "Here I am—it is written about me in the scroll—I
> have come to do your will, O God."

Through it all, the will of the Father was His primary concern.

I stand amazed!

He suffered agony in the garden, was betrayed by His own

disciple and sold for a mere pittance. He was sentenced to death on the cross by a leader who, even though convinced of Jesus' innocence, lacked the courage to stand by his convictions.

He suffered indignities of every sort, and a crown of thorns was placed on His head. Then, the death sentence was pronounced.

Isaiah had foretold it in chapter 53:3-7:

> He was despised and rejected by men,
> a man of sorrows, and familiar with suffering.
> Like one from whom men hide their faces
> he was despised, and we esteemed him not.
>
> Surely he took up our infirmities
> and carried our sorrows,
> Yet we considered him stricken by God,
> smitten by him, and afflicted.
> But he was pierced for our transgressions,
> He was crushed for our iniquities;
> The punishment that brought us peace was
> upon him.
> And by his wounds we are healed.
> We all, like sheep, have gone astray,
> each of us has turned to his own way;
> and the Lord has laid on him
> the iniquity of us all.
>
> He was oppressed and afflicted,
> yet he did not open his mouth;
> He was led like a lamb to the slaughter,
> and as a sheep before her shearers is silent,
> so he did not open his mouth.

He carried His own cross, and when He reached Golgotha, the place where He was to be crucified, it was probably dropped into the ground with a sickening thud. The torturous process of death paints a grisly picture: the blows of the hammer against splintered bone and wood as nails were driven through the hands of Jesus. Hands that had only been used for healing and soothing, for bringing in nets weighed down with fishes, for hugging a child, and feeding the hungry. One can almost hear the crowd as they hissed and jeered at the spectacle before them. I am amazed at their disregard for human suffering and their thrill at another's pain.

That dark day
        On Calvary,
You hung on the Cross;
        Humble, submissive,
        Broken, overcome with the pain
            of your suffering.
Mother, friends, followers, brothers
        Wept in bitter agony.
They felt your pain
        As though it were their own.

Mary, standing at the foot of the cross,
        Bowed down in grief.
        She saw the blood, born of her flesh,
            flowing from the tree.
She heard the sickening blows
        of hammer striking bone
            and wood.

Lord, how weak I am!
How strong You were
        That dark day on Calvary.

I often kneel at that cross
        On the hill
And feel the power of the blood
As it washes, cleanses, and purifies.

How can I ever repay
        the great debt
        of your suffering?

I stand amazed and wonder,
        How could I ever give back
        to you
What you so freely

gave to me
That dark day on Calvary?

Had I been Jesus, the Messiah, I would have done every-thing in my power to save myself. Jesus refused. He kept His eyes wide open, though in agonizing pain. He accepted it all, taking upon Himself what no other man could bear. He absorbed the shock of sins for generations past, present and future.

But the story does not end on this note of sadness and suffering. I stand amazed at the integrity of God and the fulfillment of His promises, proven through His resurrection.

> On the third day he will rise again.
>
> Luke 18:33

> Jesus answered them, "Destroy this temple, and I will raise it again in three days." But the temple he had spoken of was his body.
>
> John 2:19, 21

> After the suffering of His soul, he will see the light of life and be satisfied; by his knowledge my righteous servant will justify man, and he will bear their iniquities.
>
> Isaiah 53:11

I stand amazed...

At His Resurrection

It's the world's greatest miracle! The wonder of it all is the basis of all Christianity.

ALL of the leaders of other religions—Buddha, Hindu, Mohammad—still lie in the grave in which they were buried. But the tomb—what was to be the final resting place of Jesus—lies empty! The grave could not contain Him (Matt. 28:1-15). He was cold in death; the grave was sealed and guarded; His enemies were celebrating His death; and His friends were in mourning. Yet He arose! Man, with his great technology, has yet to bring a dead person back to life!

> But God raised him from the dead, freeing him
> from the agony of death, because it was impossible
> for death to keep its hold on him.
>
> Acts 2:24

The scenario begins with another earthquake. Imagine the wonder of Mary Magdalene and the others as they went to the tomb, expecting to see their beloved Jesus, and found the tomb empty, with nothing left but strips of linen and the burial cloth that had covered His face and head.

The apostles were astonished, and the Roman guards stood in disbelief. The Sanhedrin panicked and gave large sums of money to the guards, bribing them to tell a lie and say they were sleeping. They even bribed Pilate to keep quiet and spare the guards' lives!

Skeptics have come up with a great number of theories to disprove the fact that Jesus WAS who He said He was. They have suggested that the disciples stole the body, that the women took His body, or that perhaps they had gone to the wrong tomb. A favorite explanation is the "swoon theory," which states that Jesus was not dead, but only in a type of coma.

These same skeptics have ridiculed His teachings, denied His virgin birth, explained away His miracles and scoffed at His church, but the ONE thing that they cannot explain, account for, or deny is the resurrection of Jesus!

I stand amazed...

Because of His death and resurrection, I have been given a precious gift—one that holds great implications and fulfilled promises:

1. It means that Jesus overcame death for all people. Death is the strongest power in this world. It is the greatest weapon Satan has to use against mankind. Through Jesus' death we can know that God is stronger than death (Matt. 28:18). He is our friend and Savior, and the One alone who has the power to give us final victory!

> "Oh, how marvelous, Oh, how wonderful,
> Is my Savior's love for me."
>
> —Charles Gabriel

2. It means that since Jesus rose from the dead, I too, will rise from the dead. Jesus tried to explain this to Martha as she grieved over the death of Lazarus.

> I am the resurrection and the life. He who believes in me will live, even though he dies; and whosoever lives and believes in me will never die.
>
> John 11:25

Paul, in 1 Corinthians 15:51-54, speaks of this great promise:

> Listen, I tell you a mystery: We will not all sleep, but we will all be changed—in a flash, in the twinkling of an eye, at the last trumpet. For the trumpet will sound, the dead will be raised imperishable, and we will be changed. For the perishable must clothe itself with the imperishable, and the mortal with immortality...then the saying that is written will come true: "Death has been swallowed up in victory."

3. Since I will be raised from the dead, I will live forever! What a glorious hope this is for every Christian! It gives us a reason for being—this great assurance in Christ.

Praise God for the empty tomb!

At the Ascension

Compared to the rest of the events transpiring around the cross of Christ, this event seems to be the most miraculous of all. How I wish I had been a witness to the glory of the ascension of Christ (Mark 16:19, Luke 24:51)!

Jesus had appeared to over five hundred people in the forty days following His resurrection. On this, His last day, He led the disciples out of Bethany. He spoke to them of things to come, and as He lifted up His hands to bless them, He left this world in an amazing fashion! His body began to rise, and He was taken up into the clouds to once again be with His Father, where there would be no more Cross—no more pain—no more suffering. He sits there now, on the right hand of God, making intercession for us!

Amazing!

If I could but spend the rest of my life in gratitude and thanksgiving for the blessing of the life, death, and resurrection of Jesus, it would not be enough to repay Him for His sacrifice!

> Now to the King eternal, immortal, invisible, the only God, be honor and glory for ever and ever. Amen.
>
> Timothy 1:17

Questions

1. *What were some events surrounding the crucifixion?*

   Amos 8:9 and Luke 23:44-45 _____

   _____

   Matthew 26:24-25 _____

   _____

   Matthew 27:19 _____

   _____

   John 19:23-24 _____

   _____

   Luke 23:39-43 _____

   _____

   Matthew 27:51 _____

   _____

2. *Why did all these things happen on this certain day at this precise time?*
3. *Read Isaiah 53. Discuss each one of the prophesies of this chapter and their fulfillment.*

4. What was the significance of the "veil rent in twain"?
5. What does the Resurrection day mean to you?
6. What were some results of the Resurrection?

Hebrews 10:19-20 _____

1 Corinthians 15:3 _____

Galatians 1:4 _____

Romans 5:6 _____

Colossians 2:14 _____

7. Who are the people to whom Jesus appeared after His resurrection (1 Cor. 15:3-8)?
8. Share with the class your conception of the world as it would have been without the Resurrection.
9. What are two things the blood of Christ does for the Christian (Heb. 9:11-28)?
10. Write a paragraph paraphrase of the above section of Scripture.

Chapter 7

I Stand Amazed...
at the Grace of God

Over 250 years ago, ruthless men earned high incomes by transporting slaves across the seas. Rickety, broken-down ships carried thousands of innocent victims to foreign lands, on decks so crowded that men, women and children on board spent the entire voyage lying cramped together, body to body, unable to move, on rotten, crumbling decks, with little food or exercise. They arrived at their final destination emaciated and starved, bound by chains and ready to be sold to the highest bidder. Unless they were fortunate enough to escape, they spent the rest of their lives separated from family and loved ones, bound forever to their new masters, who often treated them with contempt and physical cruelty.

John Newton, the sea captain on one such slave excursion, encountered a violent storm at sea. Badly frightened, he turned to comfort in a book that someone had given him: *The Imitation of Christ*, by Thomas à Kempis. The words on the pages now made sense, and he was filled with remorse for the years he had spent in slave dealings. It was a different man who stepped off the ship when it docked in England. John Newton repented and spent the rest of his life preaching the good news of Christ throughout the country. To close one of his sermons, he wrote the words to the famous hymn, "Amazing Grace."

Newton's lyrics in "Amazing Grace" speak of the importance of the grace of God. Without Jesus—God's grace personified—we all stand guilty of sin, hopeless, lost, forever damned and condemned. The words describe each one of us as adults, and our certain need to seek salvation by obedience to the grace of God!

The Big Question

Grace—it's one of the most amazing, yet misunderstood words in the Bible. Repeated over 150 times, it holds center stage in the plan of God for mankind. Yet, when not fully understood, the Christian life becomes riddled with anxiety, guilt, and bondage. The concept of grace answers the most complicated question of mankind: How can God be so good to man when man is so bad to Him?

The answer can be found in John 3:16:

> For God so loved the world, that he gave his one and only Son, that whosoever believes in him shall not perish but have eternal life.

We can look to the New Testament to find the story of God's love and grace. It begins with the simple and lowly birth of a child, born into a world of sin.

> For the grace of God that brings salvation has appeared to all men.
> Titus 2:11

Jesus did not come into the world because this wicked world deserved Him. The Greek and Romans were a godless people. The Jews gave lip service to God but had no real love for Him. Throughout the ages they had rejected Him over and over again.

> Jews and Gentiles alike are all under sin. As it is written: "There is no one righteous, not even one; there is no one who understands, no one who seeks God."
> Romans 3:9-10

The world needed a Savior! We were hopelessly lost, doomed forever, and forsaken as a race without Him. We had taken all the blessings of God and the benefits of His creation. We had no way to save ourselves. Even the Mosaic law, with its rules and regulations, couldn't save mankind. Only God could accomplish the deed, and He did so through the birth of Jesus, who came to earth for the sole purpose of saving mankind.

> For the law was given through Moses; grace and truth came through Jesus Christ.
>
> John 1:17

The following poem (author unknown) describes God's gift of grace:

> If our greatest need had been information,
> God would have sent us an educator.
> If our greatest need had been technology,
> God would have sent us a scientist.
> If our greatest need had been money,
> God would have sent us an economist.
> If our greatest need had been pleasure,
> God would have sent us an entertainer.
> But our greatest need was for forgiveness,
> so God sent us a Saviour!

Grace: A Working Definition

If I want the children in my fifth grade class to understand the meaning of a difficult word, I often resort to an illustration. Ira North, minister of the Madison church in Madison, Tennessee, until his death a few years ago, told this story in a sermon he preached in 1966:

Once there was an English preacher who had been trying for weeks to clarify the concept of the wonderful, saving grace of God to his Sunday School class. One cold day in winter, he put on his coat and top hat and left the building sad in heart because many of his students did not yet understand this important doctrine.

Some boys outside the building, enjoying a snowball fight, saw the minister leave. One found his top hat too much of a

73

temptation and, throwing a snowball aimed dead center at the hat, toppled it to the ground. The minister, though angry with the boy, found this a perfect opportunity to teach the concept of grace.

The next morning he went to the young man's home and presented him with a fishing pole for his birthday.

Did the boy deserve the gift? Of course not. But it was given in love, IN SPITE OF his prankish deed. Grace is receiving something you desperately need but don't deserve.

Have you ever received a free gift notice in the mail? More than likely, it comes with strings attached, for you usually have to make a purchase or visit a resort in order to qualify for the gift. God's grace comes with NO STRINGS ATTACHED!

The New Testament is filled with stories which illustrate the grace of God shown through Jesus' walk among man. In John 8, we read the story of a woman caught in adultery. By law she stood guilty and deserved to be stoned. The teachers and the Pharisees brought her before Jesus as He was teaching in the temple court. They tried to trap Him as they asked, "We know that this sin is punishable by death—what do YOU say?"

Jesus challenged anyone who was without sin to throw the first stone. It was a quiet, subdued crowd that began to trickle from the scene, one by one, until only the woman and Jesus were left. I can imagine the Savior, standing tall and strong, placing a gentle hand on her shoulder and looking deep into her eyes as He calmly asked, "Has no one condemned you?"

"No one, sir," she answered.

He then sent her on her way, declaring, "Then neither do I condemn you. Go now and leave your life of sin (John 8:11)."

Amazing!

Paul gave his own example of grace in 1 Corinthians 15:9-10:

> For I am the least of the apostles and do not even deserve to be called an apostle, because I persecuted the church of God. But by the grace of God I am what I am, and his grace to me was not without effect. No, I worked harder than all of them—yet not I, but the grace of God that was with me.

The story of the Prodigal Son is also a beautiful illustration of grace (Luke 15). It is a revelation of the unfathomable, unalterable, amazing grace of God.

A young man ran away from home and wasted the family fortune on riotous living. After reaching the depths of poverty and despair, he started for home, where his father had forgiven him and had prepared a banquet feast in honor of his return. The father didn't say, "You have been so wicked I cannot take you back as my son." He made no conditions when the boy returned. Instead, he placed on his shoulders the best robe, put a ring on his finger, and threw a party in his honor!

This touching story demonstrates grace, shown by father, to son. The son didn't deserve it. He had done nothing to earn it. We can compare it to grace, shown by God, to mankind. We don't deserve it. We have done nothing to earn it!

Grace Versus Works

The grace of God brings into focus many questions regarding our spiritual condition. One of the prime issues under consideration in churches today is the "grace versus works" issue. Are we saved by the "work" that we do, or is God's grace sufficient for salvation?

How many times have you heard the following statements: "If ANYONE gets to heaven, she will. She has done so many wonderful works," or "That's a star in your crown!" Both statements make our entry into heaven contingent on the good deeds we do. God never meant for man to think he could merit salvation by his works!

> For it is by grace you have been saved, through faith—and this not from yourselves, it is the gift of God—not by works, so that no one can boast.
> Ephesians 2:8-9

Even Abraham could not be saved by his works:

> If, in fact, Abraham was justified by works, he had something to boast about—but not before God. What does the Scripture say? "Abraham believed God, and it was credited to him as righteousness."
> Romans 4:1-2

I was blessed to grow up in a strong, active body of Christ. The minister's messages were such that I could understand them even as a child. Unfortunately, the ones I remember the most vividly are the ones dealing with God's wrath. I remember wrestling with a feeling of intensive guilt much of the time. I never once thought as a child, and even into adulthood, that I would stand a chance of spending eternity with God! I didn't do enough good works for God! I felt that He was sitting at the door of heaven with a big feather pen writing down all the bad things I did, as well as the good things I COULD have done but did not. Good deeds brought good grades—or God's favor and grace, rather like a giant report card from God!

When I began to study in earnest the Scriptures' story of grace, I shed some of the fear and anxiety resulting from an illusion of God as an irate and angry God for whom we do good things out of grim compulsion and fear rather than love. It's a fear that feeds on a feeling of condemnation brought about by impossible demands to perform in order to please Him.

Surely there is not a soul on this earth who could do enough good works to pay God back for what He has given us! Salvation is something we DON'T have to pay for, because He already paid the price on the cross!

Accepting Grace

In order to receive the blessing of God's grace, one must stand empty and bankrupt in His presence, realizing that only through Him is salvation obtainable. Then comes believing, repenting, and proving our faith by baptism.

> Peter replied, "Repent and be baptized, every one of you, in the name of Jesus Christ for the forgiveness of your sins. And you will receive the gift of the Holy Spirit. The promise is for you and your children and for all who are far off—for all whom the Lord our God will call."
> Acts 2:38-39

> Whoever believes and is baptized will be saved, but whoever does not believe will be condemned.
> Mark 16:16

These scriptures, the backbone of Christianity, mention nothing of works being essential for salvation! Our works are done in love and are done in appreciation of salvation. We are not saved BECAUSE we do good works! Rather, we are saved TO DO good works!

For example, we hear much these days about the spiritual disciplines of study, meditation, prayer, etc. I seek to practice these disciplines. It is my privilege to understand and to embrace them. But these means of drawing near to God are given for our good, not for our bondage. They are not duties to be performed. We cannot gauge by our performance of them whether to expect God's blessings or not. They are a means to the end, but not the end themselves.

Misconceptions

This new freedom from fear of God's retribution could cause difficulty for a weak brother or sister who is looking for an excuse to sin. Such a person might say, "I'm saved! That means I can do anything!" This error can erase personal responsibility for the Christian. Such is not the case.

We have been given a gift. We must appreciate and take care of it! We are NOT free to live any way we please, no matter what the consequences. And there WILL be consequences when we live in sin!

Understanding fully the amazing grace of God means obeying His commands and living a life committed to Christ:

> Be faithful, even to the point of death, and I will give you the crown of life.
> Revelation 2:10

It means having love for your neighbor—as much love as you have for yourself (Matt. 22:37), and keeping yourself unspotted from the world (James 1:27).

It means living your life in continual, unceasing gratitude to God for rescuing you from death and giving you life. Daily we should praise and honor God for the blessings which are showered upon us each day. When I look at the cross and its significance in my life, I cannot help but bow in grateful obedience to my Lord!

As we grow older, we understand more the sacrifices our parents have made for us. Often we are called upon later in life to care for the same parents who gave us birth, fed, sheltered, and loved us. If circumstances permit, we do so out of gratitude for what they have done for us.

In the same manner, because as our faith grows we understand more of this great gift of grace, we serve God out of appreciation for Him. Things once done out of duty are done with joy and thanksgiving. Our eyes are opened to the gifts of life, love, friendship, joy, laughter, music, and a myriad of other blessings.

The following story illustrates the concept of grace:

> There was a lady who lived for twenty years with a tyrannical husband. He insisted that she maintain a perfectly clean house and made her make daily a list of chores which had to be performed before he came home in the afternoon. Each day she worked diligently, weeping from fatigue and unhappiness.
>
> This husband died, and she married another man. Out of duty and habit, she continued to perform the same chores daily. One day she looked at her list, and began to weep with great emotion, for she realized that now she was performing them out of love—not fear!

A Summary

As a child, I could not fall asleep at night until I said my prayers. I lived in constant fear that if my life were snatched away, I would spend eternity in hell if I had not prayed for my sins up to that point.

Another little girl had a different interpretation of God's forgiveness:

> I cannot believe that God forgives us for our sins as soon as we ask Him! I should think he would make us feel sorry for two or three days first. And then I should think He would make us ask Him a great many times, and in a very pretty way, too, not just in common talk. And I believe that is the way He does, and you need not try to make me think He forgives me right at once, no matter what the Bible says.[1]

She was only saying what most of us have felt on occasion. Such thoughts of despair can separate us from our loving Father more than sin itself!

One day I heard a minister liken the grace of God covering our sins to the windshield wipers on a car. When it is raining, the movement is constant, keeping the window clear so that the road ahead is visible. God's grace is constantly covering our sins, keeping the road to heaven clear. His supply is inexhaustible and exceeds the waters of all the seas on planet Earth!

What a joyous relief—a sense of freedom—to realize that I will not be perfect every moment of my life, and that God's grace will cover me through it all, as long as I am doing His will. Amazing!

> Amazing Grace, how sweet the sound,
> That saved a wretch like me.
> I once was lost,
> but now I'm found.
> Was blind, but now I see!
> —John Newton

Questions

1. In your opinion, has the church over-emphasized or under-emphasized the doctrine of grace?
2. In what ways are we to "fear" God? ("Fear God and keep His commandments" [Eccl. 12:13].)
3. Recall an incident from your childhood in which one of your parents exemplified the characteristic of grace in their dealings with you. Now remember an incident with one of your teachers.
4. Can you think of an incident in life in which you might be called upon to pause and "stoop" in an attitude or action of grace to another?
5. Read and discuss grace as explained in Romans 6.
6. What does God's grace suggest regarding our attitude towards others? Does a Christian who practices grace have any room for a judgmental attitude?
7. Discuss some inherent dangers in accepting the true meaning of grace.

8. *Discuss two other biblical examples of grace as shown in Luke 10:30 and Matthew 18:23.*

9. *Discuss Paul's testimony of grace found in 1 Corinthians 15:9-11.*

10. *Discuss what Christ meant in His statement: "My grace is sufficient for you" (2 Cor. 12:9).*

Chapter 8

I Stand Amazed...
at the Word and Its Work

It has been called:

> a lamp
> a precious treasure
> Holy book divine
> Book of life
> Truth unchanged
> heav'n drawn picture
> the Light
> the Bread of Life and
> the living Word.

These are but a few of the phrases that have been coined by poets and writers to describe the Holy Bible—the book most of us have read cover to cover at least once in our lifetime. It's found on bookshelves and bedside tables, largely ignored by some yet longed for by those who have not been privileged to turn its pages. It's the book in which the Father meets His children in love and speaks to them, imparting strength, wisdom, and power through the written Word.

Its ability to lift up man in times of stress has been proven repeatedly throughout time. In World War II, fighter pilots carried it aboard their planes, along with rations, in a waterproof bag. A copy could have probably been found in almost each of the thousands of military tents that stretched across the barren sandy deserts of the Gulf War.

Its stories grip the imagination and fire the spirit. Its words never grow old or tiresome, for each time it is read new truths are gleaned. It gives wise counsel, soothes the brokenhearted, gives bread to the hungry, strength to the weary, and hope to those in despair. Its food for the soul is the pure source of spiritual life.

Imagine a world without the Bible! One might as well drain the seas of their waters, or quench the sun and imagine the world without light, as to think that men or nations can get along without God and His Word.[1]

What makes this compilation of writings so amazing? There is no way in one chapter to cover the immensity and scope of the Holy Bible and its influence on humanity. Instead, our study will be devoted to simply looking at the remarkable background and power of the written Word.

The Bible Is Divine

The Bible is the oldest book in the world, its records embracing events from the creation of the world to the establishment of the church. It has been handed down from generation to generation; through wars and revolutions since the beginning of time. Its unifying purpose is to show how God works throughout history to make Himself known to the world and draw the world back to Himself. Its central figure is Jesus Christ.

One author writes an apt description:

> The Bible is the record of those divine break-throughs into human history. "God's search for man," it is described, rather than being our search for God...Unlike most religious literature, it is not chiefly a collection of noble sayings, but a drumroll of events, people, struggles, great and terrible, of frailty, doubts, and heroism, of the ultimate might of right. Scripture isn't meant as scientific exposition or as mere history. It is "salvation history," a universal spiritual drama of an overarching

compassion and concern for human integrity, of an unwavering love that seeks an answering affirmation. It is a vivid, sometimes parabolic account of God's persistent, unrelenting quest for us and our stumbling, often faithless response.

Its message has been scoffed at by many; yet it abides forever, miraculously preserved by God.

In this book one can find all the essentials relating to happiness and eternal safety; life, death and immortality![2]

Amazing!

The Bible Is Authentic

God's Word is reliable and valid. You can believe it! Artifacts have been dug up; ancient civilizations have been unearthed; yet nothing has ever been discovered to disprove the accuracy of Scripture. Discrepancies between its facts and scientific theory have been cleared up over and over again.

For example, years ago archaeologists discovered a ten-foot layer of mud far beneath the surface of the earth, and dug up artifacts from the Stone Age. Studies proved that the layer of clay was the residue of a vast deluge that had covered the plains of Mesopotamia around 4,000 B.C.![3] This time frame coincides perfectly with the time and location of the great flood in Noah's day.

In another incident, while excavating Babylon from 1899 to 1917, a group of German archaeologists unearthed the remains of the Tower of Babel. They estimated it equal in height to the Statue of Liberty![4] That's an amazing feat—considering that we think of ourselves as great technological wizards, able to whip up a gigantic building in less than a month with our modern equipment!

People of biblical times possessed extremely advanced scientific foreknowledge. For example, in Job 26:7, Job tells us that God "spreads out the northern skies over empty space; he suspends the earth over nothing." Centuries later men still argued over what held the earth in space!

In Isaiah 40:22, the prophet speaks of the "circle of the earth." History classes teach us that men toyed with the idea of a flat earth for 2,200 years before Magellan proved that the world was round!

Health practitioners were advanced beyond their time. In Leviticus 14, people are warned to wash their hands in running water. The concept of "quarantine" is mentioned in Revelation 14.

It almost seems supernatural! The only explanation—this book is a divine book, given by God, through men, to men!

The Bible Is Eternal

As the author of this book, I can only hope that twenty-five years from now the lessons therein will still be applicable. Because of the eternal nature of Scripture, it's possible that books such as this one might last far beyond the life span of a normal book. Other authors face the knowledge that the book they have written could possibly be dated before it comes off the press. For example, books of history are replaced periodically. Because of rapid technological advances of our society, science texts are antiquated within a few years. Yet the Bible remains indestructible!

Its message of hope is eternal. It has changed lives down through the ages. Wherever it has gone, civilization has taken root. Morals and values have been raised through better governments, schools, wives, husbands, children, employers and employees.

It stands invincible against its foes! Two hundred years ago, atheists declared that their writings would make the message of the Bible obsolete and that it would only be found in museums. Thomas Paine wrote of this in his famous pamphlets entitled "The Rights of Man," and "The Age of Reason." Later, after his prophecy failed, he regretted ever having made these bold statements regarding this seemingly indestructible book![5]

The Bible will last beyond our lifetime—beyond our children and grandchildren, on down through the annals of time!

> All men are like grass, and all their glory is like the flowers of the field; the grass withers and the flowers fall, but the word of the Lord stands forever.
> 1 Peter 1:24-25

> Your word, O Lord, is eternal; it stands firm in the heavens.
>
> Psalm 119:89

The Bible Is Inspired

> All Scripture is God-breathed and is useful for teaching, rebuking, correcting and training in righteousness.
>
> 2 Timothy 3:16

I find it amazing that forty writers of different ages, countries, and races could write sixty-six books over a period of 1,600 years and turn out a finished product containing a variety of subject matter and form, with no contradictions!

The writers of Scripture were often "unlearned and ignorant" men, each possessing a variety of temperaments, talents, and personalities. Yet every one of them, guided by the Holy Spirit to write down the words of God, wrote with complete confidence that they were speaking God's message (2 Pet. 1:21)! The result was a book of unified diversity, showing how God works through man to make Himself known to the world and draw the world to Himself.

The Bible Is Impartial

God's Word tells it like it is! It describes events as they really happened. No emotional jargon clutters the pages of this book. Even dramatic events such as the beheading of John the Baptist and the crucifixion of Christ are recorded with unemotional preciseness.

Other books gloss over flaws and imperfections in their heroes. Because the inspired writers wanted us to see the humanity of each character, they leave nothing to the imagination. David committed adultery with Bathsheba. We read the entire account, and later share his despair over his mistakes.

The Bible Gives Us Strength

> Do not be far from me, for trouble is near and there is no one to help.
>
> Psalm 22:11

Do not be surprised at the painful trial you are suffering, as though something strange were happening to you. Rejoice that you participate in the sufferings of Christ, so that you may be overjoyed when his glory is revealed....If you suffer as a Christian, do not be ashamed, but praise God that you bear that name.

1 Peter 4:12-16

Not only so, but we also rejoice in our sufferings, because we know that suffering produces perseverance; perseverance, character; and character, hope.

Romans 5:3-4

Ask any prisoner of war about his time in captivity and he will tell you that recollection of God's Word gave him strength to endure. Many have reported that when all hope was gone, verses would be brought to mind that had not been read since childhood. Many Vietnam POW's tapped out messages and verses on the wall to adjoining cellmates.

I would imagine a verse that brought strength to many was the words found in Psalm 3:

> O Lord, how many are my foes! How many rise up against me!. . .But you are a shield around me, O Lord; you bestow glory on me and lift up my head...I lie down and sleep; I wake again, because the Lord sustains me.

Anthony Bloom, in the book *Beginning to Pray*, suggests that you learn by heart those passages...

> ...that go deep into your heart, that move you deeply, that make sense, that express something which is already within your experience, either of sin, or of bliss in God, or of struggle. Then, when you are filled with despair, completely and utterly unable to call up out of your soul any spontaneous expression to God, you will find that these words

come up and offer themselves to you as a gift of God, helping your lack of strength.[6]

Several years ago, while under the pressure of finishing a book before my deadline, dealing with the stress of two teens, teaching school, weekly Bible classes, and retreats and seminars, I managed to fill every page of my calendar during the spring months. As I became more and more addled, I turned repeatedly to the calming words in Isaiah 40:28-31. Eventually I committed them to memory, where they are now stored for future needs!

> Do you not know? Have you not heard? The Lord is the everlasting God, the Creator of the ends of the earth. He will not grow tired or weary, and his understanding no one can fathom. He gives strength to the weary and increases the power of the weak. Even youths grow tired and weary, and young men stumble and fall; but those who hope in the Lord will renew their strength. They will soar on wings like eagles; they will run and not grow weary, they will walk and not be faint.

The Bible Increases Knowledge

> Your commands make me wiser than my enemies....I have more insight than all my teachers, for I meditate on your statutes.
> I have more understanding than the elders, for I obey your precepts.
> Psalm 119:98-99

Maturity comes through the searching of Scripture and real-life application of its wisdom for daily living. For example, for instructions on how to live a Holy life:

> Lord, who may live on your holy hill? He whose walk is blameless and who does what is righteous, who speaks the truth from his heart and has no slander on his tongue, who does his neighbor no wrong and casts no slur on his fellowman, who

despises a vile man but honors those who fear the Lord, who keeps his oath even when it hurts, who lends money without usury and does not accept a bribe against the innocent. He who does these things will never be shaken.

Psalm 15:1-5

How can a young man keep his way pure? By living according to your word...I have hidden your word in my heart that I might not sin against you.

Psalm 119:9, 11

The Bible Reveals God and Jesus Christ

The account of the creation in Genesis 1-3 introduces us to this God-character and reveals many of His attributes. We can learn even more by observing the universe.

By the word of the Lord were the heavens made, their starry host by the breath of his mouth. He gathers the waters of the sea into jars; he puts the deep into storehouses.

Psalm 33:6-7

The heavens declare the glory of God; the skies proclaim the work of his hands. Day after day they pour forth speech; night after night they display knowledge.

Psalm 19:1-2

The Bible reveals Christ as the only Savior (John 10:10-14:6; Matt. 1:21), and the one who loves us (Rev. 1:5-9; Acts 20:28).

The Bible Convicts of Sin and Converts the Soul

Changing lives is Jesus' business, and He accomplishes His task through the power of the Word. God's Word is like a mirror. Looking into our reflection, we can see the dirt and clean it off. Reading the Word, we see wherein we fail, and we clean up our life.

Therefore no one will be declared righteous in his sight by observing the law; rather through the law become conscious of sin.

Romans 3:20

I am not ashamed of the gospel, because it is the power of God for the salvation of everyone who believes: first for the Jew, then for the Gentile. For in the gospel a righteousness from God is revealed.

Romans 1:16-17a

By this gospel you are saved, if you hold firmly to the word I preached to you. Otherwise, you have believed in vain.

1 Corinthians 15:2

People the world over are hungering for the Word. World Bible School has shipped over 100,000 Bibles in the last twenty years to Nigeria and Africa, and demands far exceed the manpower necessary to follow through. People in Russia are hungry for the Bible and now have the New Testament available. All over the world souls are being converted to Jesus Christ through the reading of His Word. A church building is not necessary—nor are Bible teachers. Just the simple Word of God.

My Response

I have no other guide to immortality and eternal life. Jesus has spoken. His is the Word. Ours is the obedience.

To give any less than my devoted attention to the study of Scripture is to take away from God Himself. Simply reading the Word is not sufficient.

One author writes:

Many Christians remain in bondage to fears and anxieties simply because they do not avail themselves of the discipline of study. They may be faithful in church attendance and earnest in fulfilling their religious duties and still they are not changed....They may sing with gusto, pray in the Spirit, live as obediently as they know, and yet the tenor of their lives remains unchanged. Why?

Because they have never taken up one of the central ways God uses to change us—study. Jesus made it unmistakably clear that it is the knowledge of the truth that will set us free.[7]

There is only one thing of any lasting value on this earth, and that is the way to heaven. God Himself has condescended to teach me the way. He wrote it down in a book—a book which deals with certainty on life, death and eternity.

In *A Room Called Remember*, Frederick Buechner gives one of the most moving summaries ever written of this amazing book:

> The Bible is hundreds upon hundreds of voices all calling at once out of the past and clamoring for our attention like barkers at a fair, like air-raid sirens, like a whole barnyard of cockcrows as the first long shafts of dawn fan out across the sky. Some of the voices are shouting, like Moses, so all Israel, all the world, can hear, and some are so soft and halting that you can hardly hear them at all, like Job with ashes on his head, and his heart broken, like old Simeon whispering, "Lord, now lettest thou thy servant depart in peace." The prophets shrill out in their frustration, their rage, their holy hope and madness; and the priests drone on and on about the dimensions and furniture of the Temple, and the lawgivers spell out what to eat and what not to eat: and the historians list the kings, the battles, the tragic lessons of Israel's history. And somewhere in the midst of them all one particular voice speaks out that is unlike any other voice because it speaks so directly to the deepest privacy and longing and weariness of each of us that there are times when the centuries are blown away like mist, and it is as if we stand with no shelter of time at all between ourselves and the one who speaks our secret name. "Come," the voice says. "Unto me. All ye. Every last one."[8]

Amazing!

Questions

1. How is God's Word described in these verses?
   Jeremiah 23:29
   John 6:63
   Ephesians 6:17
   Hebrews 4:12
2. How do the writers of Scripture attribute their words to God in the following passages?
   Deuteronomy 28:1-2
   2 Samuel 23:1-3
   Jeremiah 1:6-9
   1 Thessalonians 2:13
3. What importance does God place on His Word (Psa. 138:2)?
4. How did Jesus use Scripture in the following situations?
   Mark 7:6-9
   Mark 12:24-27
   Luke 10:25-28
5. What else did Jesus have to say about the Scriptures?
   Matthew 5:17-18
   John 17:17
6. What do you find out about God and His nature through the account of creation in Genesis 1-3?
7. If a person in a foreign country were to get the New Testament, could he or she decide what to do to be saved without the guidance of a preacher or institution?
8. Study carefully Psalm 119. List at least five benefits of God's Word.
9. This week memorize at least one verse or as much as one chapter of Scripture.
10. Share with the class your favorite Scripture and explain its relevance to your life.

Chapter 9

I Stand Amazed...
at the Spirit,
God's Special Gift

In the movie *Star Wars*, the good guys believed in a mysterious force which guided them and protected them in the struggle between good and evil. They encouraged each other with the words, "May the force be with you." Likewise, there is a mysterious force which dwells in God's people. This force is more powerful than dynamite and as invisible as electricity! It has more power than the wind and the sea. It has been called the "breath of God" and the "water of life." It is God's Spirit!

It is unfathomable that God, the Father, expressed His love in so many ways: the gift of Christ; the beauty of the Creation; the love, care and concern of others; but also through His own personal representative—the Holy Spirit!

> And hope does not disappoint us, because God
> has poured out his love into our hearts by the Holy
> Spirit, whom he has given us.
> Romans 5:5

It's with great trepidation that I begin this chapter, for I know so little about walking in the Spirit. I have just begun my acquaintance with this special friend. Why I have not realized earlier in my walk that this mysterious force truly exists—that He is a living, moving force in my existence—is an amazing phenomenon, considering that Scripture abounds with evidence of His existence AND proof of His work in the lives of Christians. The Word is very precise and clear about our life in His Spirit. Over and over He urges us to walk in the Spirit, to give Him entrance into our lives.

Learning more about Him is an exciting quest—one that will take you deeper than ever before into the heart of Jesus. It will take some element of self-discipline to break through preoccupation with human trappings and stand stripped and exposed before Him. As I have, you will learn that the more you study, the more there is to discover! And the more you discover, the greater will be your hunger to get to know this special friend and helper!

In order to simplify your study, the lesson will be approached much from the same angle that a reporter writes a story about a special person or event—always including information on the "Who, What, Where, When, and Why."

Who and What is the Holy Spirit?

1. The Holy Spirit is a distinct personality. He's not a vapor, or a phantom ghost like you see on Halloween. He's not an imaginary vague hope. He's not a heavenly breeze or a hazy cloud floating in and out of your life.

Jesus called the Spirit "He" in John 16:8, "When He comes He will convict the world."

2. He is the third person of the trinity. He is equal to God, the Father, and Jesus.

> Therefore go and make disciples of all nations, baptizing them in the name of the Father and of the Son and of the Holy Spirit.
>
> Matthew 28:19

3. He knows everything!

> For who among men knows the thoughts of a man except the man's spirit within him? In the

same way no one knows the thoughts of God except the Spirit of God.

1 Corinthians 2:11

Why the Holy Spirit is Here

It's difficult to accept the fact that something is gone...vanished...done away with. When we lose a loved one, it is not part of our reality system to believe that that loved one will return at some time or another or that he is living on in our own body. The apostles of Christ had to believe such a thing. They experienced deep anguish when Jesus broke the news of His upcoming death. They could not understand the words with which He tried to comfort them:

> You may ask me for anything in my name, and I will do it. If you love me, you will obey what I command. And I will ask the Father, and He will give you another Counselor to be with you forever—the Spirit of truth. The world cannot accept him, because it neither sees him nor knows him. But you know him, for he lives with you and will be in you.

John 14:14-17

Though saddened more than their words could express when the reality of Calvary was raised before them, after the great events on Pentecost (Acts 2), when Jesus sent the Holy Spirit into the heart of the disciples, we can find no record of them ever regretting the absence of the physical presence of Jesus. When He walked on earth, He could only commune with one of them at a time. His crowded schedule left them little time for fellowship. They longed for time alone to commune with their dear friend and teacher.

Now, after the imparting of the Holy Spirit, they found His presence in their lives at all times, whether they were together in Jerusalem or scattered about in different parts of the world. The wonder of it all is that He has promised us the same thing— His very presence empowering us to live the Christian life!

All of us have two parts—a natural part and a spiritual part. With the gift of the abiding Spirit, we experience a divine spark deep within which eventually affects an amazing metamorphosis in our lives. We are changed into the very likeness of God. We like the same things, we have the same love for others, and we have the same goals as did Jesus, our Lord.

Without God's Spirit, the natural part of us reigns supreme. We grow up to become egocentric, animal-like creatures who "look out for number one" and have no regard for others. Saddam Hussein and Hitler are two perfect examples of men who have lived their lives without the presence of the Holy Spirit. You can see the results of similar lifestyles in the ghettos and the cultures of many non-Christian countries.

His purpose is real. It's everlasting. It's amazing!

Where Is the Holy Spirit?

HE IS OMNIPRESENT. He can be in all places at the same time. He is just as real in Nashville, Tennessee as He is in Moscow. David, in Psalm 139:7-8, says:

> Where can I go from your Spirit? Where can I flee from your presence? If I go up to the heavens, you are there; if I make my bed in the depths, you are there.

HE IS IN OUR BODY! He actually comes into my body to reside! If God asked you for a design of a personal dwelling place for Him what would you create? A place of solitude on a high hill? Among the clouds? On the wings of the wind? A majestic cathedral? Your own frail body? Never!

My body is more than a place where I house vital organs; more than an external shell that houses me. It's the place that God lives! The dwelling place of God Almighty! The sanctuary for the Almighty God!

> Do you not know that your body is a temple of the Holy Spirit, who is in you, whom you have received from God?
>
> 1 Corinthians 6:19

Isn't this thing called the Holy Spirit a great and exciting mystery?

When and How Does the Spirit Work?

Many people believe the Holy Spirit still works in the same way today as in the apostolic period, but a careful examination of the scriptures reveals that the methodology has changed. Paul tells us in 1 Corinthians 13:10 that the age of miracles would cease but that the Spirit would continue to work though Christians to produce the "perfect love" which is the essence of God. He is working in our lives at this very moment. His responsibilities are so many that one might say He has a ministry of "assistance."

1. The Spirit is involved in our maturing process. There would be no need for the Spirit if we could be holy on our own strength. But we can't stand alone. We need help in the quest for Holiness. He teaches me truth through God's own Word, which He Himself inspired! When I am in despair over a situation, He takes the circumstances in my life and gives me insight. He brings Christ to me. He is my teacher, helper, and friend. He transforms me and leads me in the path of right living. He assures me of the presence and power of Christ in my life.

> But when He, the Spirit of truth, comes, He will guide you into all truth. He will not speak on his own, he will speak only what he hears, and he will tell you what is yet to come. He will bring glory to me by taking from what is mine and making it known to you. All that belong to the Father is mine. That is why I said the Spirit will take from what is mine and make it known to you.
>
> John 16:13-15

He might be called the Great Illuminator. He does not draw attention to Himself, but focuses attention on Christ and our Father.

2. The Spirit protects us. In early Rome, a governmental seal on a document was evidence of Roman ownership and protection. When we are sealed with the Holy Spirit, it means that we are protected by God and identified as His because we have the "seal" of His Spirit.

> Having believed, you were marked in him with a
> seal, the promised Holy Spirit, who is a deposit
> guaranteeing our inheritance until the redemption
> of those who are God's possession—to the praise of
> his glory.
>
> Ephesians 1:13-14

The Holy Spirit is also a deposit, or down payment. When I purchase an item on credit, I often have to make a down payment in order to assure that I will fulfill my responsibilities. Later, on a monthly basis, I pay off my debt.

God's Spirit has been given to us as a down payment. The rest will come later, when we walk through the gates into the arms of the One whom we have lived for! I start that process, and the Spirit empowers me to complete it one step at a time.

3. The Spirit makes us more Christ-like. The inner working of the gracious Spirit produces a mind marked by the qualities of the mind of Christ. When we are "born again" in the water and spirit, three things occur in our lives. Our sins are forgiven, God adds us to His church, and He bestows upon us a precious gift—the gift of His Spirit (Acts 2). Just as a baby is born with the genes and chromosomes from his parents, God's children are born with an invisible spirit which causes them to grow and mature into the image of their heavenly Father.

John wrote,

> Because you are sons, God sent the Spirit of his
> Son into our hearts, the Spirit who calls out "Abba,
> Father."
>
> Galatians 4:6

We can't see or feel this indwelling force just as a baby can't see its genes, but when he is grown people will comment on the remarkable resemblance between the father and the son or the daughter and her mother. None of us fully understands it, and we may live the Christian life for years before we become aware of it, but we accept it through the eyes of faith. Yes, we are possessed! Not by some demonic spirit from hell but by the third person in the holy trinity—God's Divine Spirit.

We can't see electricity, but we can see the effects of electric current every time we turn the lights on. Similarly, the fruits of God's Spirit, though invisible, are each a dynamic, living function of the very love of God. Paul wrote,

> The fruit of the Spirit is love, joy, peace, patience, kindness, goodness, faithfulness, gentleness and self-control.
>
> Galatians 5:22

These are the characteristics of a spirit-filled life. They are what differentiates me from Saddam Hussein. They also describe the very nature of God. As Christians mature in their walk with God, they become more and more like their Father. This is an amazing process which occurs quietly over the years but is the inevitable consequence of a life with God.

He does not force us to be holy, but is forever present in our lives, reminding us of Christ and our call to discipleship. Whenever we are moved to do a good deed for another, the Spirit is working. Whenever we forgive, He is present. Whenever our spirit soars with joy, the Holy Spirit is deep within the heart. Whenever we are with friends and are transformed from our usual grouchy self into a kind loving human being, He is there.

4. The Spirit helps us pray. In order for any relationship to grow and mature, communication must take place. This includes our relationship with God. Prayer is our means of communicating with Him. In Hebrews 4:16, the author tells us of the special privilege we have in prayer:

> Let us then approach the throne of grace with confidence, so that we may receive mercy and find grace to help us in our time of need.

J. Oswald Sanders wrote:

> The Spirit links himself with us in our praying and pours His supplications into our own. We may master the technique of prayer and understand its philosophy; we may have unlimited confidence in the veracity and validity of the promises concerning prayer. We may plead them earnestly. But if

we ignore the part played by the Holy Spirit, we have failed to use the master key.[1]

There are two dimensions to prayer: what you contribute, and what the Holy Spirit contributes without your knowledge. Many times my mind is so cluttered I cannot concentrate on prayer. At others times the words simply cannot express my desires. At such times the Holy Spirit becomes my partner in prayer. He intercedes for me—to God—and offers up prayers which I could not utter.

> In the same way, the Spirit helps us in our weakness. We do not know what we ought to pray for, but the Spirit himself intercedes for us with groans that words cannot express. And he who searches our hearts knows the mind of the Spirit, because the Spirit intercedes for the saints in accordance with God's will.
> Romans 8:26-27

> And pray in the Spirit on all occasions with all kinds of prayers and requests.
> Ephesians 6:18

In the highest sense, prayer is communion with God. It is in the fellowship of the Spirit. It gives constant assurance, quiet strength, and serene stability.

In Conclusion

There's no better time than now to begin your quest for an understanding of the Holy Spirit. Once you begin, you won't be able to turn away, for what you have tasted of in this brief lesson is but the beginning of the mystery and magnificence of this holy guest.

When you get to know Him, you won't hear voices rumbling out of the stormy skies. You WILL be aware of a new ability to overcome sin, to be free from worry and stress, and to live a life of victory as a Christian. With the Holy Spirit in your life, you will be more sensitive to God and His plan for your life. You will be refreshed, reshaped and renewed—with a new vitality for positive living!

It's amazing!

Questions

1. When does the Holy Spirit enter your life?
2. Why hasn't the church emphasized more the role of the Holy Spirit in the life of a Christian?
3. How do we know that the Spirit does not work miraculously through Christians today?
4. What are some results of the Holy Spirit's presence in the life of the believer (2 Tim. 1:7)?
5. The Holy Spirit has been called fifty-seven names in the Bible. How many can you name?
6. Discuss the baptismal measure of the Spirit.
   Matthew 3:11
   Luke 24:49
   Acts 10:44; 11:15-16
7. What does the term "indwelling" of the Spirit mean?
   Acts 2:38
   Acts 5:32
   Galatians 4:6
   Romans 8:9
   1 Corinthians 6:18-19
   Ephesians 1:13-14
8. The Spirit works in numerous ways. Discuss those found in 2 Peter 1:5-11 and Romans 8:11.
9. Whom does the Holy Spirit glorify?
10. What personal characteristics will you see in the lives of people who are filled with the Spirit?

Chapter 10

I Stand Amazed...
at Love, the Greatest Gift

Once upon a time, in a small village, there lived a woman and her two children. Destitute save for the clothing on their backs, they had barely enough food to get them through the day, and their shelter was but a small wooden hut with a dirt floor. One day the hut caught on fire, and when the woman found that escape was impossible, she dug a hole in the dirt floor and placed her children there, covering them with her body. When villagers came to fight the fire, the hut was almost completely destroyed. They found the mother, burned and charred beyond recognition, and her two small children—alive.

Love is the most amazing and powerful of all human emotions. A mother's love will deny and even sacrifice self if called upon to do so. As parents, we can understand that kind of love. But God's love is beyond human comprehension. It is undeniable and unexplainable. It transcends all knowing.

Long ago an explorer attempted to measure the depth of the ocean in the far North. He kept a record of his attempts. Each day he had to lengthen his instrument. Each day he wrote, "Deeper than that." One day he fastened all his lines together and let them down into the sea. His entry was still the same: "Deeper than that." He finally gave up all attempts.

The love of God is like that ocean. It is like the limitless expanse of the universe. It has no boundaries. Its riches cannot be exhausted.

Amazing!

> To write the love of God
>> Would drain the ocean dry,
>> Nor could the scroll
>> Contain the whole
>> Though stretched from sky to sky.
>>> —Selected

Another poet expressed it like this:

> Could we with ink the ocean fill,
>> And were the skies of parchment made,
> Were every stalk on earth a quill
>> And every man a scribe by trade;
> To write the love of God above
>> Would drain the ocean dry;
> Nor could the scroll contain the whole,
>> Though stretched from sky to sky.

Love That Lasts

God's love is everlastingly eternal, poured out in unrelenting power upon mankind.

> God says, "I have loved you with an everlasting love."
>> Jeremiah 31:3

One of the great Old Testament words for love is *hesed*. It is often translated as "steadfast, constant" love. It focuses on the permanence of the relationship God has with the people to whom He has committed Himself. He genuinely cares about us and what happens to us. There are times when we are plunged into a pit of blackness, filled with overwhelming despair and loneliness. Perhaps there is a feeling that no one cares. At such times we need to be reminded of the constant and tender concern of the One who loves us in an "unearthly" kind of way.

In the book of Hosea, there is a beautiful, intimate picture of God's constant and tender care:

I took my people up in my arms,
I drew them to me with affection and love,
I picked them up and held them to my cheek;
I bent down to them and fed them.

Hosea 11:3-4

A Love That Gives

God's love for His children manifests itself in many ways. Just as we do things to delight and please our loved ones, so did God desire to bring pleasure to His children, and so He created Planet Earth with its amazing beauty and color, its delicate intricacies and details. Each season bears its own proof of God's love, for He has sent us gift after gift of pleasure to look upon and experience: from the deep, silent wonder of the midnight sky to the pounding restlessness of the sea; from the fragile delicacy of snowflakes in winter to the thundering fury of a mighty storm; from the grandeur of the mountains to the gentle breeze of a forest meadow. All are gifts of God, bestowed freely upon His children because He loves them! What a dismal world He could have created. Instead, He chose to please us and to reveal himself in His creation.

We marvel at the millions of kinds of life in the world, especially the human body, so perfectly made, and the mind that is able to think great thoughts and plan great deeds. We have to reason that all these things did not just happen, that behind all creation there must be a supreme being who is great, wise, and all-powerful. There must be One who loved us enough to bring into existence this world of ours and to create a plan for our redemption.

This amazing love is what we sing about in "The Wonder of It All:"

There's the wonder of sunset at evening,
The wonder as sunrise I see,
But the wonder of wonders that thrills my soul
Is the wonder that God loves me.

There's the wonder of springtime and harvest
The sky, the stars, the sun;
But the wonder of wonders that thrills my soul
Is a wonder that's only begun.

O the wonder of it all!
The wonder of it all!
Just to think that God loves me,
O the wonder of it all!
The wonder of it all!
Just to think that God loves me!

—George Beverly Shea

A Redeeming Love

God's greatest demonstration of His love was when He left the splendors of heaven in the form of a man, to suffer in ways that most of mankind will never experience.

John wrote about this gift in John 3:16:

> For God so loved the world that he gave his one and only Son, that whoever believes in him shall not perish but have eternal life. For God did not send his Son into the world to condemn the world, but to save the world through him.

God the Father's majestic body, in the form of Jesus Christ, was broken on our behalf, crucified on the cross, spilled out in self-sacrifice for our salvation.

> But we see Jesus, who was made a little lower than the angels, now crowned with glory and honor because he suffered death, so that by the grace of God he might taste death for everyone.
> Hebrews 2:9

He loved ME enough to die for ME! He loved me enough to want me to spend eternity with Him. When we love something enough, we will pay any price to get it....

Once a young boy made a toy boat. It brought him many hours of joy. One day he was sailing it on a small lake and the wind began to puff at the tiny hand-formed sails, causing the boat to drift further and further from the grasp of its creator. He was heartbroken, for he thought he would never see the boat again. Then, one day he was walking through town and spotted it in the window of a toy shop. He had no money to purchase his treasure, but worked for weeks at small jobs until he had

106

earned enough to walk into the store, pay the owner, and finally hold it in his hands. He wept with happiness as he said, "I made you and now I bought you back."

And so God made us, and He buys us back through the price of death of His beloved Son.

A Jesus Kind of Love

While He walked on earth, Jesus Himself manifested the love of God. It broke through every barrier of race, creed, color, occupation, and beliefs. It's the kind of love that we desire to emulate. It sets us apart as children of God, changes our lives and shows the world that we belong to Jesus. It makes us easier to BE loved.

UNCONDITIONAL AND UNSELFISH

Jesus' love never said "if" or "because." It never expected anything in return. If you love those who love you, what credit is that? How are you different? If you love those who don't love you in return, there's grace in that (Luke 6:32-35).

Jesus knew exactly how to begin a relationship. He didn't just SEE people, but accepted them wherever they were. It didn't matter how unlike Him the person was, or how difficult. He found their needs. He sought their suffering. He saw those things that were locked up inside them, screaming for release.

His love didn't stop with the outside of a person, but looked beyond, into the heart, and drew aside their faults and imperfections like the pulling back of a curtain. It's the kind of love I wish I could have for those people who prickle my skin and intrude upon my comfort zone. I wish I could look at them through the eyes of Jesus, with the mask removed, the scales dropped off. This is the kind of love that releases the person to grow. It gives them freedom and unlimited possibilities.

SERVING AND SACRIFICIAL

Jesus was constantly hanging Himself on little crosses— knowing that what He was about to do was going to cause someone to get angry and would cause Himself emotional pain. He healed the crippled man on a Sabbath, knowing that He was going to raise the hackles of those who opposed Him. He sacrificed Himself for a person in need.

Self-sacrifice is often easy to do for those we love. It is not so easy for the others—like those who sought to have Jesus put to death, or those who pounded the nails into His hands and jeered at His cries of agony.

Have you ever had the experience of something nasty coming your way and someone else taking it upon himself? That's exactly the kind of love Jesus had for mankind. He sought suffering. I run from it. Yet I once read, "When Jesus calls a man, He calls Him to cry." That's what love is all about.

We will never love God's people until we've been to the foot of the cross. We'll never find out how much we love God until He asks us to do something we don't want to do. We'll never discover the remarkable power of love until we're called upon to sacrifice self for another.

I am reminded of the sacrificial love of Jesus when I recall a story from the Special Olympics for handicapped children at Vanderbilt University in Nashville. Many of the entrants didn't really understand the physical competition. They were simply caught up in the excitement and fellowship of the moment. On different occasions, one in the lead would turn around, see a friend faltering, and turn back. They would then join hands and run together.

A flock of geese soaring on the wind exhibit the same spirit of serving. They fly in the shape of a "V" because of the extreme physical exertion caused by blasting into opposing wind currents. When they grow weary, the ones in the front move to the back while others relieve them.

That's the kind of love Jesus had. If we can emulate it, it's a love that shows we are all part of a great tie that binds us to Christ and to one another.

The Loftiest Kind of Love

If you've ever experienced the beauty of "agape" love, you've tasted a little bit of heaven on earth. It's a love that sees the highest good of another. It refuses to respond negatively, reject, demand, or judge another. It exhibits itself when you take the back seat although you'd rather have first-place honor. It creeps out when your physical and mental energy say "No more!" It comes through when you minister to the hurts of others and when you laugh even though it would feel better to cry. When you can love like this, you have reached the lofty heights of God-love.

How Sweet, How Heav'nly

How good God was to us that He instilled in each human being the same capacity for love as He Himself had! Without it, we as a people are doomed. Love can mend fences, bind together nations, unite a family, and bring peace to war-torn lands. It can move us to feed the poor and give shelter to the homeless. With it we can love the unlovely and care for the sick. Love binds together our fellowship of believers.

> How sweet how heavenly is the sight,
> When those that love the Lord,
> In one another's peace delight,
> And so fulfill the word.
>
> When each can feel his brother's sigh,
> And with him bear a part,
> When sorrow flows from eye to eye,
> And joy from heart to heart.
>
> When love in one delightful stream
> Thro' every bosom flows;
> When union sweet and dear esteem
> In every action glows.
>
> Love is the golden chain that binds
> The happy souls above.
> And he's an heir of heav'n who finds
> His bosom glow with love.
> —William Bradbury

Just as the breakers of the ocean waves come crashing unendingly upon the shore, so does the love of God come sweeping over my soul moment upon moment. There is no possible way to repay Him except to love and serve others. God is more impressed with our goodwill and selfless love than with any other sacrifice we might make. He has called us to be large in spirit, generous and great-hearted toward others, extending mercy and kindness to all with whom we come in contact.

> A new command I give you: Love one another.
> As I have loved you, so must you love one another.
> By this all men will know that you are my disciples,
> if you love one another.
>
> John 13:34

> Dear friends, let us love one another, for love comes from God.
>
> 1 John 4:7

> No one should seek his own good, but the good of others.
>
> 1 Corinthians 10:24

Dale Carnegie relates the following simple basic requirement of human life:

> I shall pass through this world but once.
> Any good, therefore, that I can do,
> Or any kindness that I can show to any human being,
> Let me do it now.
> Let me not defer it, or neglect it,
> For I shall not pass this way again.
>
> —Author unknown

Robert Browning wrote of this amazing love of God:

> God, thou art love!
> I build my faith on that.
> I know Thee who has kept my path, and made
> Light for me in the darkness, tempering sorrow
> So that it reached me like a solemn joy;
> It were too strange that I should doubt Thy love.

We need to come to Christ and drink deeply of His love. There we can find refreshment and reinvigoration in His consistent care!

Questions

1. In John 10:9-16, Jesus compares His love and concern to the love and concern of a shepherd. According to this passage, what are some things He wants to give to you?

2. 1 Corinthians 13 focuses the reader's attention on the meaning and importance of love. Think of all the different ways you can summarize what love is, then compare your definition with verses 4-7.

3. What resources can you draw upon to enable you to love like God?

4. In your own words, write down what Jesus wants to do to express His love to you as a Christian, based on Ephesians 5:25-27.

5. Read Romans 8:28-39. List what this passage teaches you about the results of your love for God and God's love for you.

6. Discuss Jesus' friendship with His disciples. Was it unconditional or conditional? Discuss the reasons for your answer.

7. Realizing that Jesus has loved you, how can that affect your relationships with those you find hard to love?

Chapter 11

I Stand Amazed...
at the Glory of God's Church

Last year, my husband's grandmother died at the mature age of ninety-four. She had ten children, forty grandchildren, and more than a hundred great-grandchildren and great-great-grandchildren. The people who gathered in the church for the afternoon funeral came from states across the nation. They wore many different surnames and could not identify half the people there. As in most families, some held grudges against other family members and had not spoken in years. Yet they all had one thing in common—all were related by birth or by marriage to the deceased. They were family!

I believe heaven will be like that. All of God's children gathering from the four corners of the earth. All of different ages and from totally different circumstances; a huge throng of strangers with only one thing in common—their relationship to the Father. When they meet, it will be as though they have known each other a lifetime, for they are the true blood "kinship" of God. Revelation 7 describes a scene very similar to this. One of the elders asked John, "Who are all these people and where did they come from?" The heavenly elder had to answer his own question. "They are those who have been washed in the blood of the lamb."

Amazing, isn't it? In this huge gathering, all came in through the same door—the blood of the Lamb! The entrance is the church of Jesus Christ our Lord.

113

The Called Out

In Matthew 16, Jesus asked His disciples who they thought He was. Peter was right on target when he answered, "You are the Christ, the Son of the living God." Jesus replied, "On this rock I will build my church, and the gates of Hades will not overcome it." The Greek word for "church" in this passage is *ekklesia* which simply means "the called out" or "the called together."

God calls His family out of the world—from the four corners of the globe, from the teeming masses of the cities to the remotest jungle village, young and old, black or white. He reaches down into the ranks of humanity and draws people to Himself and places them all together into one big spiritual family—His church. This body was established to accomplish His eternal purpose—the salvation of man. The church exists because it was His intention to create a people for Himself who would serve Him and obey His will.

> The church's one foundation is Jesus Christ Her Lord,
> She is His new creation, by water and the word.
> From heaven He came and sought her
> To be His holy bride;
> With His own blood He bought her,
> And for her life He died.
> —Samuel J. Stone

The word "church" is used in two senses in the New Testament: the universal church, or all those washed in the blood who accept Jesus as head; and a word used to designate a specific congregation that meets together to break bread. The second sense is simply a sub-set of the first. The church is God's saved family—on earth and in eternity. What a glorious creation!

Roots

I am amazed when I think of the origin of the church. How spellbinding it would have been to be an eyewitness to the miracles of Pentecost: the great gushing of a violent wind; tongues of fire separating the people and resting on each of them, filling the apostles with the power of the Holy Spirit! What a scene to witness!

114

When the day of Pentecost came, they were all together in one place. Suddenly a sound like the blowing of a violent wind came from heaven and filled the whole house where they were sitting. They saw what seemed to be tongues of fire that separated and came to rest on each of them. All of them were filled with the Holy Spirit and began to speak in other tongues as the Spirit enabled them.
Acts 2:1-4

In one giant climactic act of faith, 3,000 people repented, received the Word, and were washed in the blood of the Lamb— all in one day.

Those who accepted his message were baptized, and about three thousand were added to their number that day.
Acts 2:41

And thus began the church of our Lord. Those who were baptized into Christ came from many different nations and spoke different languages, but they were joined together by one common bond—the blood of Christ.

The apostles had no say in who was added—no vote, no veto, no judgment. Everyone was added to the same church and there was only one. They had no building, no minister, no eldership, no worship committee, and no organized youth group! They were instantly part of God's family, held together by a common bond of love in Christ.

Without delay, filled with the fire of the Spirit, they poured into the streets of Jerusalem, fearlessly declaring their faith, teaching, caring for one another, breaking bread, and praying (Acts 2:42). Their message spread rapidly and new members were constantly added to their numbers.

They devoted themselves to the apostles' teaching and to the fellowship, to the breaking of bread and to prayer. Everyone was filled with awe, and many wonders and miraculous signs were done by the apostles. All the believers were together and

had everything in common. Selling their possessions and goods, they gave to anyone as he had
need. Every day they continued to meet together
in the temple courts. They broke bread in their
homes and ate together with glad and sincere
hearts, praising God and enjoying the favor of all
the people. And the Lord added to their number
daily those who were being saved.

Acts 2:42-47

Just as He had planned it from the beginning! Amazing!

Courage and Commitment

I am amazed at the courage and commitment of the early
church. These brave new Christians lived under the threat of
persecution from day one, for the Jewish establishment was
not about to tolerate a popular new sect in their holy city. Much
to the consternation of the emperor, people all over the Roman
Empire were buying into it. There were small pockets of
believers in every imaginable place—from the elaborate
temple and synagogues to private homes. No longer safe
worshipping in public, believers were finally forced into hiding
and driven to distant places (Acts 4-8).

There's a long roll call of those who marched into persecution and martyrdom. Peter and John were called before the
Sanhedrin and threatened—then arrested and jailed. Stephen
was stoned to death outside of Jerusalem. Paul, the fearless
evangelist, was flogged repeatedly, imprisoned, starved, stoned,
shipwrecked, and possibly finally beheaded by the Roman
authorities. It is probable that all of the apostles except John
became martyrs for the cause of Christ. He was banished in
exile for his beliefs.

Imagine the Superdome filled to overflowing with tens of
thousands of screaming fans, all gathered to view not a bowl
game, but a ceremony whose purpose is to annihilate Christians. It was a common scene in Rome as the persecution
became massive. Christians were crucified by the thousands—thrown to wild beasts, or burned as human torches in
Nero's courtyard. Under the emperor Domitian (95 A.D.),
more than 40,000 Christians were tortured and slain. Throughout the reign of ten or more emperors, approximately seven

million Christian martyrs were murdered for their belief in Jesus Christ and buried in the Catacombs of Rome. Yet the church grew and even thrived as three generations of Christians, driven into new regions by the heat of persecution, were willing to give their lives for Christ rather than renounce their Lord!

Amazing!

It is impossible for Christians today, living in religious freedom, to identify with the courage of our early brothers and sisters. The hardest thing many of us have ever had to do is miss a ball game to worship with the local church. Would the church today be as large if we, as believers, had to die for our faith?

Unity

I am amazed at the unity of the church. It is as Christ desired:

> My prayer is not for them alone. I pray also for those who will believe in me through their message, that all of them may be one, Father, just as you are in me and I am in you. May they also be in us so that the world may believe that you have sent me. I have given them the glory that you gave me, that they may be one as we are one: I in them and you in me. May they be brought to complete unity to let the world know that you sent me and have loved them even as you have loved me.
>
> John 17:20-23

The Jerusalem church continued to evangelize and grow. Much of their success in the community could be attributed to their faithfulness and unity. Although there was diversity, not only the Jerusalem church but Christians of many nations were united on the essentials listed in Ephesians 4—one body, one Spirit, one hope, one Lord, one faith, one baptism, and one God. Down through the centuries, God's church surfaced in various forms and at various places, but the same essential beliefs were shared.

Elect from every nation, yet one o'er all the earth,
Her charter of salvation, One Lord, one faith,
    one birth.
One holy name she blesses, partakes one holy food,
And to one hope she presses, with every
    grace endued.
                                        —S. J. Stone

Today, God's true church exists wherever believers observe one baptism into the one Lord. Christians may disagree over a thousand different points of doctrine, but there is one common thread that joins us together—the precious blood of Christ. Paul said in Acts 20:28 that Christ purchased the church with His own blood. In spite of different customs, languages, races, educational levels, or social rank, Christians everywhere share many of the same characteristics. They are all related to the same Father.

Simplicity

I am amazed at the simple structure of the church. Paul addressed the Philippian letter to the elders and deacons in the local church, giving them explicit guidance on how to lead the flock. We find no other structure in the New Testament—no world headquarters, no national conferences, no regional dioceses, no state convention center, no head bishop, no hierarchy, no ecclesiastical pecking order, legislature or constitution. Just a plurality of elders or shepherds looking after each local flock!

There are no citizenship requirements. No race of people have a natural advantage. The church unites all believers from every race, tribe, color and language in a common ministry in Christ and a common hope for Christ's return.

The 21st Century Church

One day my two-year-old got into my knitting ball and tangled the yarn into a jumbled mess. She brought it to me in tears and said, "Sorry, Mommy, it's all messed up."

The Christian community today resembles that tangled ball of yarn. Factions of God's modern-day church have argued and divided over various doctrines and opinions until there are more than three hundred separate entities all claiming to be God's family. Only God can straighten out the mess! He alone knows who His true children are and will forgive us for our foolishness. He alone knows our intent was good even if the end is disappointing. Jesus once said,

> I am the good shepherd; I know my sheep and my sheep know me—just as the Father knows me and I know the Father.
>
> John 10:14-15

Jim Woodruff, in *The Church in Transition*, says that "our only hope of being a part of a living, life-giving movement is to be called back to the exalted Christ who lives and breathes in the Gospel records."[1] That's the church that God intended from the beginning. That's the church that amazes me!

> Mid toil and tribulation, and tumult of her war,
> She waits the consummation of peace for evermore;
> Till with the vision glorious, her longing eyes are blest,
> And the great Church victorious shall be the Church at rest.
>
> —S. J. Stone

Questions
1. Discuss the difference in the way the term "church" was used in the first century and the way we use it today.
2. Why did the early church suffer so much persecution? What would happen to the church of today if Christians faced persecution by the government?
3. How is a person added to the church today?
4. Is it necessary for members of the church to agree on everything in order to have unity in Christ?
5. What institution does Paul compare Christ and the church to in Ephesians 5:23?
6. How is it possible for the church to be "without spot or blemish" when it is made of up sinful people (Eph. 5:27)?

7. *Does the church "roll" we keep on earth have any meaning to God?*

Chapter 12

I Stand Amazed...
at the Hope of Glory

> When with the ransomed in glory,
> His face I at last shall see.
> 'Twill be my joy through the ages,
> To sing of His love for me.
> —Charles H. Gabriel

Imagine the most majestic scene you have ever witnessed on land or sea. Imagine a place with the brilliance of a dazzling, priceless jewel, bathed in the tender and radiant splendor of God, the Father. Loud Hosannas and praise fill the air with spontaneous and genuine worship as the redeemed of the ages and the angels in unending fellowship pay tribute to the glory of Him who reigns in majesty.

Language is inadequate to express it. Mortal mind is incapable of imagining it. It's light! Music! Beauty! Joy! It's a life of unending splendor which God has prepared in heaven—where the redeemed soul finds never-ending peace with God! There is no darkness, no evil, no sins, tears or regret. Earthly existence with its limitations and imperfections is no longer. Spiritual existence is flooded with eternal bliss in this dwelling place of God almighty!

Not all the archangels can tell
The joys of that holiest place
Where Jesus is pleased to reveal
The light of His heavenly face.
—Charles Wesley

God's work from the beginning of time amazes me. However, there is nothing that He did or ever will do that can compare to the glory of heaven!

A City of Gold?

When I was a child, I thought of heaven as a great shining city with golden walls and domes and streets and soaring spires, with angels floating ethereally through the golden streets. Now, I associate heaven with people, with things of lasting beauty, and with praise songs filling the air. I envision a state of complete beauty, for I rejoice in the beautiful things of this world.

I have no sound doctrine to verify such a description—for Scripture does not give us an exact detailed account of heaven. John, in Revelation, gave us a brief glimpse, but the language is figurative. He, too, attempted to describe it in terms of those things which symbolized preciousness—dazzling jewels, streets of shining gold, etc. No mortal mind with its finite limitations could understand the magnitude and glory of heaven. That is as God planned it!

No eye has seen,
No ear has heard,
No mind has conceived
what God has prepared for those who love him.
1 Corinthians 2:9

I wish I could have been Paul, who was given a brief glimpse of glory. It was enough to make him wait for the rest of his life on the edge of expectancy, eager to go at any moment!

I am torn between the two: I desire to depart and be with Christ, which is better by far; but it is more necessary for you that I remain in the body.
Philippians 1:23

122

Until Glory, we will not know what Paul saw in that brief moment. Not having been given that precious glimpse, we form our own conception of what heaven is like. Each of us paints a picture in the mind and holds it close. Uniquely individual, each differs from another's. We don't dwell on the logistics, nor the details. We simply breathe in the heart-felt wonder at a God who loved us enough to prepare a place where we can be with Him forever. We accept it on simple faith.

Up, Up, and Away!

We can know that heaven is up. It's beyond the atmosphere, the troposphere, even beyond the planets and the solar system. It's beyond the far galaxies—beyond the billions and billions of stars in the heavens.

> For the Lord himself will come DOWN from heaven, with a loud command, with the voice of the archangel and with the trumpet call of God, and the dead in Christ will rise first. After that, we who are still alive and are left will be caught up together with them in the clouds to meet the Lord in the air. And so we will be with the Lord forever.
> 1 Thessalonians 4:16-17

> God looks DOWN from heaven on the sons of men to see if there are any who understand, any who seek God.
> Psalm 53:2

> After this I looked, and there before me was a door standing open in heaven. And the voice I had first heard speaking to me like a trumpet said, "Come UP here, and I will show you what must take place after this."
> Revelation 4:1

Although our knowledge is limited, there is no doubt in my own mind that heaven is "above the deep blue, the beautiful blue."

I love to stand on the top of a tall mountain, or to fly high above the clouds. Astronauts who have traveled in outer space say they have "touched the face of God." Heaven is in another dimension—one beyond human understanding. When we try to imagine heaven, we are tempted to give it an ethereal, dreamworld quality. Or, perhaps we see a massive Disney World complex floating in and out among the clouds!

Perhaps we will all be greatly surprised to find that this new home, which encircles the entire world, solar system, galaxy and universe, is very stable, secure, and permanent!

Home of the Soul

In 2 Corinthians 5:1, Paul mentions that if our earthly body is destroyed, we inherit an eternal home from God. *Home.* It's a word that brings feelings of warmth, acceptance, security, and love. To most it symbolizes permanence.

I've lived in this place I call home now for eight years. It's the most permanent dwelling I have known since I married a minister-husband-professor twenty-five years ago. Throughout our years together, our homes have been mostly temporary. In the first ten years of our marriage we moved eleven times! I felt like a permanent pilgrim and stranger! I couldn't plant flowers or trees, nor attach anything permanent to a home that could at any moment belong to someone else.

In today's mobile society, most of us are not allowed the luxury of putting down roots. The American Dream has made it thus. We must move on to bigger and better things—so we pack up the U-Haul and start out on move #10.

God has planned better things, for the home He is preparing for His true believers will not be temporary. It's eternal and secure!

> Praise be to the God and Father of our Lord Jesus Christ. In his great mercy he has given us new birth into a living hope through the resurrection of Jesus Christ from the dead, and into an inheritance that can never perish, spoil or fade—kept in heaven for you, who through faith are shielded by God's power until the coming of the salvation that is ready to be revealed in the last time.
>
> 1 Peter 1:3-5

It is a home for the soul—that part of us which we cannot see or touch or feel but lies at the base of all our thoughts and inner workings. It will be our dwelling place down through the ages. Into eternity. Forever and ever. It can never perish, nor spoil, nor fade. It has been prepared—perhaps is still being prepared—with loving care and concern for the happiness and welfare of the children of God. Jesus ascended to the Father to prepare for His followers to join Him there.

> Do not let your hearts be troubled. Trust in God; trust also in me. In my Father's house are many rooms; if it were not so, I would have told you. I am going there to prepare a place for you. And if I go and prepare a place for you, I will come back and take you to be with me that you also may be where I am.
>
> John 14:1-3

Here, without using the word "heaven," Jesus captures the essence of a prepared place for prepared people called His Father's house.

What a Fellowship!

Old friends and acquaintances, loved ones who have passed on, friend greeting friend and souls who have long been separated are united! How the heavenly corridors must ring with rapturous joy as loved ones and friends reunite!

How sweet the joy! The essential joy of heaven, however, will be its abode with the Father and its fellowship with the Son. God the Father (John 14:1-6), the Son (1 Cor. 15:23-25) and the Holy Spirit will be there. Just think of being with Deity eternally and of seeing God face-to-face!

Think of talking with all of God's people throughout the ages! World figures, beloved Bible characters, poets, scholars, and martyrs. All will be resting in a joyous communion of saints in heaven. Nothing is more uplifting and energizing than to sit around a table filled with food and enlightening conversation! What a fellowship we will share in heaven! In reading through Hebrews 11 we can get a small glimpse into heaven's Hall of

Fame—all of whom will be readily accessible to share the great mysteries of all times with God's fellowship of believers!

Matthew described it in chapter 25:31-32:

> When the Son of Man comes in his glory, and all the angels with him, he will sit on his throne in heavenly glory. All the nations will be gathered before him.

Jesus spoke of the great gathering and fellowship in Matthew 8:11:

> I say to you that many will come from the east and the west, and will take their places at the feast with Abraham, Isaac and Jacob in the kingdom of heaven.

A Far Better Place

All I have to do is pick up the morning newspaper or tune in to any news channel to discover how many troubles have invaded this world. Murder, abuse, drugs, AIDS, the homeless, a faltering economy, broken homes; the list could go on and on. Hardly a family has not been touched by one disaster or another in recent years.

Life has enough troubles for all of us plus more! Job expressed, "Man born of woman is of few days and full of trouble (Job 14:1)." And 1 John reveals, "We know that we are children of God, and that the whole world is under the control of the evil one (1 John 5:19)." Yet God's Word tells us that our suffering is infinitely small compared to the glorious inheritance God has for us.

Paul described it in Romans 8:18:

> I consider that our present sufferings are not worth comparing with the glory that will be revealed in us.

He continues the thought:

> We ourselves, who have the firstfruits of the Spirit, groan inwardly as we wait eagerly for our

adoption as sons, the redemptions of our bodies. For in this hope we were saved.

Romans 8:23-24

For He has rescued us from the dominion of darkness and brought us into the kingdom of the Son he loves, in whom we have redemption, the forgiveness of sins.

Colossians 1:13-14

We might call it a "Prelude to Glory." That's all our sufferings are—a prelude to the wonder God has in store for us in heaven. Not only will our present earthly sufferings cease, but in heaven we will no longer be shackled and bound by a mortal body. Those who are aging or who suffer from terminal illness or crippling disease will be released from their agony as they take on a new body, clothed in immortality!

How much better will be our abode in heaven! Paul writes of it in 2 Corinthians 5:1-5:

> Now we know that if the earthly tent we live in is destroyed, we have a building from God, an eternal house in heaven, not built by human hands. Meanwhile we groan, longing to be clothed with our heavenly dwelling, because when we are clothed, we will not be found naked. For while we are in this tent, we groan and are burdened, because we do not wish to be unclothed but to be clothed with our heavenly dwelling, so that what is mortal may be swallowed up by life.

The apostle Paul had nothing physical on this earth. He was 100% dependent on God and longed for the joys of heaven. He wrote of these feelings in Philippians 1:21-24:

> For to me, to live is Christ and to die is gain. If I am to go on living in the body, this will mean fruitful labor for me. Yet what shall I choose? I do not know! I am torn between the two: I desire to depart and be with Christ, which is better by far.

How different it is for us today! We have everything a soul could want—which makes it difficult for us to imagine how Paul felt as he longed for a place where things could be better.

Death—the Final Victory
The most amazing thing about this place called heaven is that God could have deserted us at death to the grave. He could have left this mortal body to rot in the ground. We would fight it out, get sick and die. Instead, He cared enough to share His home in heaven with us to redeem us from spiritual death and physical death. Oh, the wonder of it all! Christ arose from the dead, affirming His victory over sin and death!

> But Christ has indeed been raised from the dead, the firstfruits of those who have fallen asleep. For since death came through a man, the resurrection of the dead comes also through a man.
> 1 Corinthians 15:20-21

> For this reason we should never become discouraged. Even though our physical being is gradually decaying, yet our spiritual being is renewed day after day. And this small and temporary trouble we suffer will bring us a tremendous and eternal glory, much greater than the trouble. For we fix our attention, not on things that are seen, but on things that are unseen. What can be seen lasts only for a time; but what cannot be seen lasts for ever.
> 2 Corinthians 4:16-17 (TEV)

To die in Christ is to live in eternal spiritual union with Him! It is a departure for eternal fellowship with Christ! It is the first step and the ONLY step that takes us into the arms of our Lord.

Seneca, an ancient philosopher, said, "That day which you fear as being the end of all things is the beginning of your eternity."

Martin Luther wrote:

> What is our death but a night's sleep? For as through sleep all weariness and faintness pass away and cease, and the powers of the spirit come

128

back again, so that in the morning we arise fresh and strong and joyous; so at the Last Day we shall rise again as if we had only slept a night, and shall be fresh and strong.

Victor Hugo said:

> The tomb is not a blind alley; it is a thoroughfare.
> It closes on the twilight, it opens on the dawn.

All that we really need to know about heaven is that Christ is there. In tenderness and splendor, His presence is full and sufficient assurance of a blessed, abundant life. This is death in perspective. Death transformed by the resurrection of Jesus Christ as part of God's great redemption.

Jesus said:

> I tell you the truth; whoever hears my word and believes him who sent me has eternal life and will not be condemned; he has crossed over from death to life.
>
> John 5:24

For a glorious passage on the resurrection of the body, read 1 Corinthians 15:35-37, 42-44, where Paul answers the question, "How can the dead be raised to life?" What kind of body will they have?

> But someone may ask, "How are the dead raised? With what kind of body will they come?" How foolish! What you sow does not come to life unless it dies. When you sow, you do not plant the body that will be, but just a seed...So will it be with the resurrection of the body. The body that is sown is perishable, it is raised imperishable; it is sown in dishonor, it is raised in glory; it is sown in weakness, it is raised in power; it is sown a natural body, it is raised a spiritual body.

Is it such a great mystery? No more, says Paul, than that of the dry seed planted in the ground which brings forth its fruit in its season. He goes on to describe the glorious mystery of resurrection:

> We will not all sleep, but we will all be changed—in a flash, in the twinkling of an eye, at the last trumpet. For the trumpet will sound, the dead will be raised imperishable, and we will be changed. For the perishable must clothe itself with the imperishable, and the mortal with immortality. When the perishable has been clothed with the imperishable and the mortal with immortality, then the saying that is written will come true: "Death has been swallowed up in victory."
>
> > "Where, O death, is your victory?
> > Where, O death, is your sting?"

There is much yet to be said on the subject of death, heaven and the glorious resurrection. Certainly much of it is beyond our understanding and must be accepted on simple faith.

Lyman Abbott, an ancient mystic, wrote:

> I neither know nor wish to know what the future life has for me. I would not, if I could, stand at the open window and peer into the unknown beyond. I am sure that He whose mercies are new every morning and fresh every evening, who brings into every epoch of my life a new surprise, and makes in every experience a new disclosure of His love, who sweetens gladness with gratitude, and sorrow with comfort, who gives the lark for the morning and the nightingale for the twilight, who makes every year better than the year preceding, and every new experience an experience of His marvelous skill in gift-giving, has for me some future of glad surprise which I would not forecast if I could.[1]

The wonder of it all is too great—the glory too dazzling! It brings a deep, new longing to the heart and a glad anticipation to the soul!

Questions

1. Share with the class your personal conception of heaven.
2. After reading 2 Peter 3:9, what would you pinpoint as the single most important reason for all that God does for us both physically and spiritually?
3. List and discuss what we must do in order to qualify for eternal life.
4. Who has the greatest confidence of sharing in Christ's glory according to Romans 8:17?
5. Examine heaven in the account of a man raised from the dead—a man who came back from beyond—in John 11.
6. What can we know about the second coming of Christ from Matthew 24:42-44?
7. Name some ways you can reveal your readiness for that day.
8. Discuss what happens to the body at death (2 Cor. 5:8) and at the final judgment (Rev. 20:11-15).
9. How can we KNOW that we will spend eternity in heaven (John 10:9)?

Chapter 13

I Stand Amazed...
at the Beauty of Worship and Praise

When I touch the velvet softness
of a simple rose
or feel the rough texture of bark
on an ancient oak...
When I smell the summer rain
on a field of flowers,
or hear the crashing symphony
of the pounding surf...
When I view the miracle of life and love,
and the myriad mysteries
of Creation;
When I gaze with wonder
upon children of my flesh
become man and woman,
When I realize that I have security
not only in this world,
but in the world to come...
My heart fills to overflowing with delight
and gratitude to the Creator
of it all!

David, warrior, king, shepherd, and the master of poetic praise and worship, could express it so much more beautifully:

> Praise be to you, O Lord, God of our father Israel, from everlasting to everlasting. Yours, O Lord, is the greatness and the power and the glory and the majesty and the splendor, for everything in heaven and earth is yours. Yours, O Lord, is the kingdom; you are exalted as head over all. Wealth and honor come from you; you are the ruler of all things. In your hands are strength and power to exalt and give strength to all. Now our God, we give you thanks, and praise your glorious name.
>
> 1 Chronicles 29:10-13

As an author, I find that some chapters are more difficult to write than others. I research, write, edit, rewrite, and discard page after page of manuscript trying to get the message across. There are other chapters which seem to flow with the ease of sand in an hourglass. So it is with this lesson on praise and worship. It's as though I've been preparing to write it for a lifetime. From the first time I thrilled to the words of "How Great Thou Art" on a star-studded evening at summer camp to the present, praise has been a vital part of who I am and what I stand for.

In *How to Triumph Over Trivia*, I wrote of my first snowmobiling adventure in Colorado five years ago. During that frightening but exhilarating drive to the top of a six-thousand-foot mountain on a trail carved through ten-foot drifts of snow and around endless hairpin curves, I found myself singing joyful praises to God in a spirit of joyous celebration. Those songs and my feelings were a natural human response to the Divine.

At that moment, I might have penned along with David the words of praise found in Psalm 95:1-7:

> Come, let us sing for joy to the Lord;
> Let us shout aloud to the Rock of our salvation.
> Let us come before him with thanksgiving
> and extol him with music and song.

For the Lord is the great God,
    the great King above all gods.
In his hands are the depths of the earth,
    and the mountain peaks belong to him.

The sea is his, for he made it,
    and his hands formed the dry land.

Come, let us bow down and worship,
Let us kneel before the Lord our Maker;
For he is our God and we are the people
        of his pasture,
    the flock under his care.

A Heritage of Praise

The Greek word for worship is *proskuneo*, which translated means to "fall down with the face to the ground in humble adoration." It is an outpouring of love, gratitude and joy—an intimate connection with the living God. If you have ever experienced the height of such adoration and praise as you meditate upon the glory of God, then you have tasted a bit of heaven here on earth. Men and women of God down through the eons of time have shared those same feelings, moved by God's character and His intervention on their behalf.

After the historical deliverance of the children of Israel in the parting of the Red Sea, Moses and the Israelites sang a song of praise in Exodus 15:

I will sing to the Lord,
for He is highly exalted.
The horse and its rider
    he has hurled into the sea.
The Lord is my strength and my song,
    he has become my salvation.
He is my God, and I will praise him,
    my father's God, and I will exalt him. . .

Who among the gods is like you,
    O Lord?
Who is like you—
    majestic in holiness,

awesome in glory,
working wonders? . . .

The Lord will reign
for ever and ever.

Hannah, rejoicing over the birth of her long-awaited and prayed-for child, Samuel, gave us one of the most elevated praise poems of the Bible in which she praises the justice, power and sovereignty of God:

> My heart rejoices in the Lord; in the Lord my horn is lifted high. My mouth boasts over my enemies, for I delight in your deliverance. There is no one holy like the Lord; there is no one besides you; there is no Rock like our God.
>
> 1 Samuel 2:1-2

Mary, upon finding she was to bear the Christ-child, sang in adoration:

> My soul glorifies the Lord
> and my spirit rejoices in God my Savior...
> For the Mighty One has done great
> things for me—
> Holy is his name.
>
> Luke 1:46, 49

The Power of Worship and Praise

Nothing should supercede the worship of God's people—whether it be private or corporate. It has forever been a part of God's plan for His redeemed and serves several purposes:

1. Worship glorifies God, and extols His character and worth. Our God is the only true God. His infinite power and goodness leave us speechless in His presence, for He is our Creator and Redeemer! Only He is mighty in His Sovereign power over all the earth. He made us in His image, and He is our shepherd. His faithfulness remains steadfast. Such character calls us to respond with praise and worship!

The true nature of worship is to give, not to receive. It's the "hugs and kisses" we give to God. We often approach worship in a "what am I going to get out of it?" mode, rather than a time of praise and adoration. In true worship we see God high and lifted up.

Psalm 66:4-8 describes His glory:

> All the earth bows down to you; they sing praise to you, they sing praise to your name. . .Praise our God, O peoples, let the sound of his praise be heard.

How can we help but respond to His perfectionism and provision with such words as found in Revelation 5:12-13:

> Worthy is the Lamb, who was slain, to receive power and wealth and wisdom and strength and honor and glory and praise!. . .To him who sits on the throne and to the Lamb be praise and honor and glory and power for ever and ever!

2. Worship moves us to service.

> How can I say thanks for the things you've done for me?
> Things so undeserved that you've done to prove your love for me?
> The voices of millions of angels cannot express my gratitude.
> All that I am and all that I ever hope to be;
> I give it all to you because you are worth all that to me.
> —Sung by Andrae Crouch

The desire to repay kindness and love is a natural human response. God has done so much for me—surely there is but something I can do to return to Him a small portion of His goodness toward me. It is this genuine longing to serve that is an act of true worship.

Out of my body flows the essence of Christ! I am to take that body, which houses the soul and the spirit, and send a sweet aroma before God—through the channels of obedience, prayer and worship, through deeds, through justice and mercy for others, and through creativity. I am to take the invisible God and make Him visible through my life. I am to release the Savior through my body, to serve anywhere, any way— expressing to God what He is worth.

Every segment of my life is a praise song to the Creator! When I focus on Him in worship and praise and respond with a sincere desire to serve, I am reminded that all that I am and all that I do is simply a means to glorify God.

> Therefore, I urge you, brothers, in view of God's mercy, to offer your bodies as living sacrifices, holy and pleasing to God—this is your spiritual act of worship.
>
> Romans 12:1

3. Worship refreshes the spirit and enhances my daily walk. One of the major purposes and end results of a true worship experience is renewal. Renewal for a restless spirit, for a soul burdened by the demands of day-to-day living, and for a heart which yearns for communion with God.

Just last Sunday we visited a congregation whose entire service was dedicated to praise and celebration of God. The hour began with Scriptures of praise read with reverence and dignity, interspersed with praise songs. The minister's message directed the heart to the goodness and greatness of God and the miracle of the cross. A natural flow into the Lord's Supper with songs and readings gave meaning to the service, which ended with more praise and thanksgiving. Announcements for the congregation had been reserved up to that point, so that nothing would destroy the beauty and continuity of the message of the Cross. I left with a renewed sense of God's power and majesty which remained with me throughout the week.

Meaningful worship experiences with God provide memories which encourage and empower God's people during times worship is not possible. At the Passover, on the first day of the

Feast of Unleavened Bread, Jesus desired to commune with His disciples. He chose a room in which to meet with them and to tell them of coming events. Saddened and under the shadow of death, they closed their meeting with a song before going out to face the world (Mark 14:26).

Do our songs send the name of Jesus into our days of trouble? Does what happens around the table at worship lead us out into the world, better prepared to face whatever might happen, with Jesus on our lips and in our hearts?

Several years ago I discovered a beautiful praise poem and copied it onto the front page of my Bible. Its message focuses my mind so beautifully on Christ as I prepare to worship:

> Eternal God, from whom streams every impulse
>   that is beautiful and true,
> Help us in this hour of worship to take grateful
>   inventory of what sustains us;
> The friendships.
> The shared goals.
> The intimate labors that lace life with meaning.
> We thank you for music,
>   and for everything that elevates our spirits
>   above the smoggy confusion of our time
>   and gives us hope.
>
> Remind us that to every gift there is attached a
>   responsibility.
> To every privilege an obligation.
>
> Therefore, make it our purpose
>   as it is yours throughout the universe,
> To bring creativity rather than chaos,
>   harmony rather than discord,
>   talent and appreciation
>   rather than cynicism and apathy.
>
> Arrange our sympathies into your symphony,
> O Lord in whom we trust,
>   and in whose grace we
>   are never confounded.
>   —Source unknown

Suggestions for Praise and Worship

Determine to improve your praise life, for God is worthy of your best efforts!

Find praise in the ordinary. Discover fragments of loveliness in the daily events of life! Open your eyes and sense the wonder! Learn to recognize it in its most daily and mundane forms—the first snow of winter, the stillness of a summer's eve, the sound of gentle rain on the dry, parched earth.

Listen for the refreshing exclamations and excitement of children. Listen to God's voice which often speaks in silence, for stillness, quiet, and rest in the spirit are essential to a life of praise and worship. Unplug the television, turn off the stereo, and wait!

> "Be still, and know that I am God"
> Psalm 46:10

Use the still quiet hours of the night to praise and worship. If you find yourself unable to sleep, start at the beginning of the alphabet and think of ways to praise God!

Praise Him through poetry and music.

> Sing praises to God, sing praises;
> sing praises to our King, sing praises.
> Psalm 47:6

The word "praise" can often be literally translated in musical terms. Music can often move the spirit within when all else is shut out. In Hebrews 12:2, "in the presence of the congregation I will sing your praises," might be translated "I will hymn thee."

Explore the poetry of David and other inspired writers, as well as the praise and prayers of the ancients whose very lives were expressions of praise. Use other sources of praise, for authentic prayers can be formulated with words given by other people. There are published guides available. Use portions of Scripture to celebrate the nature of God. Great prayers of the Bible can be committed to memory and used when our own power is limited. Often we are immersed so deeply within ourselves and the burdens that surround us that it becomes virtually impossible to focus on God! At such times it is helpful to turn to the writings of others, Scripture, or a hymn to inspire and encourage us to greater thoughts of God.

Commit to a spirit of giving rather than receiving. When we attend a worship service, it is to give to God—not to see what we can "get out" of it. Approach it with a positive spirit, thinking such thoughts as, "Worship is going to be **good** today because I have something good to offer up to God."

Be tolerant and considerate of the styles and tastes of others. It is virtually impossible for a worship leader to meet the needs of every person in the congregation. Some like ancient hymns, others worship best with contemporary songs. Some like foot-stomping gospel music, while others are moved by devotional songs. Some find congregational reading and praise quite edifying. Others prefer a single reader. Three songs, a prayer, Scripture, the Lord's Supper, and then the sermon might be perfectly satisfactory to some, while others might find diversity each week a refreshing energizer.

A worship leader should be aware of the rich variety of ways people can offer up their praise to God. Doing the same thing without diversity for a period of one hundred years can often dull the spirit of the participant! If that is the case—in a very kind way suggest practical changes which might better meet the needs of the entire congregation.

A New Song

Society beckons us to a world of greed and materialism. God calls us to a life of praise. Through focusing on Him, we can become a part of that which will continue throughout all eternity—part of the endless discovery of God Himself. We can lift our voices thousands of times over in a doxology of thanksgiving. We can turn our eyes upon Jesus and our faces toward His altar, waiting in quiet peace and filled with praise in His presence, for...

> He put a new song in my mouth,
> a hymn of praise to our God.
> Psalm 40:3

> Giver of life, creator of all that is lovely,
> Teach me to sing the words to your song;
> I want to feel the music of living

And not fear the sad songs
>   But from them make new songs
>   Composed of both laughter and tears.

Teach me to dance to the sounds of your world
>   and your people,
I want to move in rhythm with your plan.
Help me to try to follow your leading
>   To risk even falling
>   To rise and keep trying
Because you are leading
>   the joyous celebration
>   dance of life!

—Author Unknown

Questions

1. Discuss what it means to worship God in "spirit and in truth."
2. Often we're hindered in efforts to praise by a lack of focus on proper priorities. Discuss the story of Mary and Martha in Luke 10 and its significance to today's society.
3. Discuss the following statement: "Praise opens the door toward God in such a way that we are freed for true worship."
4. Were the habits and customs of Bible times more conducive toward generating praise?
5. Discuss the role of praise in one's prayer life.
6. How can we more effectively center our worship services on praise and celebration?
7. What are some disqualifications or hindrances to genuine worship—both private and corporate?
8. How can praise bring renewal?

Endnotes

Chapter 1

1. George Barna, *The Frog in the Kettle: What Christians Need to Know About Life in the Year 2000* (Ventura, CA: Regal, 1990), 50-63.
2. Tim Hansel, *You Gotta' Keep Dancing* (Elgin, IL: Cook, 1985), 57.
3. G. W. Target, "The Window," from *The Window and Other Essays* (Mountain View, CA: Pacific, 1973), 5-7.

Chapter 2

1. J. B. Phillips, *Your God is Too Small* (New York: Macmillan, 1964).

Chapter 3

1. Edith Schaeffer, *The Art of Life* (Westchester, IL: Crossways, 1987), 21.
2. Veronica Zundel, ed., *Eerdmans' Book of Famous Prayers* (Grand Rapids, MI: Eerdmans, 1983), 85.

Chapter 4

1. Glenn Clark, *I Will Lift Up Mine Eyes* (New York: Harper, 1937), 18.

Chapter 5

1. *Disciples' Study Bible, NIV,* notes on Luke 2 (Nashville, TN: Holman, 1988).
2. Fulton Sheen, *Life of Christ* (New York: Doubleday, 1977).

Chapter 6

1. Gordon McDonald, *Forging a Real-World Faith* (Nashville, TN: Nelson, 1989).

Chapter 7

1. Hannah Whitall Smith, an excerpt from writings in *Christian Classics* (Grand Rapids, MI: Eerdmans, 1985), 95.

Chapter 8

1.Walter Knight, *Knight's Treasury of Illustrations* (Grand Rapids, MI: Eerdmans, 1963), 12.
2.George Cornell, *The Untamed God*, taken from *Disciplines for the Inner Life* by Bob Benson and Michael W. Benson (Nashville, TN: Nelson, 1989), 127.
3.Walter Knight, *Knight's Treasury of Illustrations*, 12.
4.*Knight's Treasury*, taken from *Time*, 29 Oct. 1956, 18.
5.Walter Knight, 18.
6.Anthony Bloom, *Beginning to Pray* (Ramsey, NJ: Paulist, 1970), 116.
7.Richard Foster, *Celebration of Discipline* (New York: Harper, 1978), 62.
8.Frederick Buechner, *A Room Called Remember* (New York: Harper, 1984), 128.

Chapter 9

1.J. Oswald Sanders, *Spiritual Leadership* (Chicago: Moody, 1967), 79.

Chapter 11

1.Jim Woodruff, *The Church in Transition* (Searcy, AR: Bible House, 1990), 35.

Chapter 12

1.Lillian Wichler Watson, ed., *Light From Many Lamps* (New York: Simon & Schuster, 1979), 57.